Food for Life

...and other dish

Food for Life

...and other dish

Edited by

Lawrence Schimel

CLEIS
PRESS

Published in the United States by Cleis Press Inc., P.O. Box 8933, Pittsburgh, Pennsylvania 15221, and P.O. Box 14684, San Francisco, California 94114.

Printed in the United States.
Cover design: Pete Ivey
Book design: Karen Huff
Logo art: Juana Alicia

First Edition.
10 9 8 7 6 5 4 3 2 1

"Breakfast Cush Cush" © 1995 by RuPaul, first published in *A Musical Feast*, edited by Wendy Diamond, Global Liaisons Incorporated. Published by permission of Global Liaisons Incorporated, Wendy Diamond, Karin Flores, and the author.
"Cornbread" © 1987 by Jewelle Gomez, first published, in an earlier form, in *Turning the Tables* by the Sheba Collective.

Most of the recipes contained in this book have been tested and edited from their original form. Some recipes have been maintained in their original form to reflect the personality of the artist who contributed the particular recipe. Cleis Press, the organizations who are the beneficiaries of this book, the editor, and contributors take no responsibility for any liability arising out of any injury of any kind which may be sustained from participation in or connection with the making or utilization of the recipes included in this publication.

Library of Congress Cataloguing-in-Publication Data

Food for Life & other dish / edited by Lawrence Schimel. — 1st ed.
    p. cm.
  Includes index.
  ISBN 1-57344-061-2 (pbk.)
  1. Cookery. 2. Celebrities. 3. Gays. I. Schimel, Lawrence.
TX714.F662 1996
641.5—dc20   96-36131
                                         CIP

Acknowledgments

The publication of any book owes much to the effort of many people; this book benefitted from the help, advice, and support of many, each of whom has my gratitude. In particular, special thanks are due:

To Frédérique Delacoste and Felice Newman for recognizing the importance of this project.

To Leasa Burton, for her patience and for not freaking out when this manuscript arrived in such a disastrous state.

To Deborah Barkun and Charity Denlinger for helping bring the book, and its message, to the widest possible audience.

To PGW, for their dedication and commitment to this project.

To Richard Labonté for invaluable assistance and advice, with helpful kibbitzing from the staffs of A Different Light in New York and San Francisco.

To Michael Denneny for moral support and suggestions.

To Nancy Faulconer, Karin Flores, and Tess Timony for their help nagging on my behalf and their help in acquiring some of the recipes.

To Jill Hornick and John Boone for late-night brianstorming at the eleventh hour.

To Alysía Abbott for assistance that bailed me out at half past the eleventh hour.

To Wendy Diamond, publisher of *A Musical Feast*, a cookbook benefitting the National Coalition for the Homeless, Empty the Shelters, Coalition for the Homeless—New York, and Coalition on Homelessness San Francisco, for her generosity and her own dedication. Copies of *A Musical Feast* may be ordered by calling 1-800-420-4209.

To Royal Fraser for expanding my culinary horizons and sharing so many meals (and not letting me get out of washing up afterwards!)

To my father for his cookbook collection, and his agitating for me to do a queer cookbook.

And, of course, to all the contributors, who donated their support, time, names, and recipes to this project.

The Menu: Table

Introduction • 9
Organization • 11
Nutrition and HIV • 11

Getting Wet: Soups 13

Turkish Red Lentil Soup • *Paul Russell* • 15
Dream Soup • *Patricia Nell Warren* • 16
Chicken Rice Stew • *Cecilia Tan* • 20
Swami Shankara's Squash and Cumin Soup, Hot or Cold • *Gavin Geoffrey Dillard* • 22
Grandma Ruthie's Chicken Soup for Very Special People • *Lesléa Newman* • 24

Everything That Rises: A Baker's Half Dozen 25

Breakfast Cush Cush • *RuPaul* • 27
Johnny Cake • *Marion Dane Bauer* • 28
Cornbread • *Jewelle Gomez* • 30
Tea-Time Scones • *Stephanie Rosenbaum* • 32
Tomato Bread • *Thom Gunn* • 34

Drag for Food: Dressings and Marinades 35

Pesto • *Martina Navratilova* • 37
Whatever • *Aiden Shaw* • 38
Garlic Mud for Self-Lovers • *Betty Dodson* • 40
Fail-Safe Salad Dressing • *Stephen McCauley* • 42
Seduction-Salad Dressing • *Gerry Gomez Pearlberg* • 44

The Naked and the Noodle: (Ad)Dressing Pasta 47

Trés Gay Lasagna • *Michael Musto* • 50
Mock Gourmet Clam Sauce Linguini • *Lucy Jane Bledsoe* • 52
Laura's Never Fail, Amazingly Rich & Chunky Tomato Sauce • *Laura Antoniou* • 54
Anti-Vampire Garlic Pasta with Fresh Herbs • *Pam Keesey* • 56
Mary Louisa • *Tony Kushner* • 58

Everything but the Girl: Fish 61

Seafood Paella • *Achy Obejas* • 63
Lobster Salad for Jim Owles • *Lawrence D. Maas* • 66
Everything but the Grill • *Ellen Kushner* • 68
Smoked Salmon and Hazelnut Fettucine • *Carol Queen* • 70

# of Contents

Chicken and Other Jailbait: Poultry and Eggs 71

Prelude to Decadence: Dinner for a Date in Under Fifty Minutes • *Kitty Tsui* • 75
A Perfect Dinner Party in Two Hours • *Michael Denneny* • 78
Mami's Coke Soy Chicken • *James Johnstone* • 80
Newmas Duck • *Nancy Garden* • 82
Soft Breakfast Tacos • *Lars Eighner* • 85
Queering the Quiche • *Victoria A. Brownworth* • 86

Beefcake: Playing with Your Meats 91

The Loaves-and-Fishes Almost-Any-Meat (But No Fish) Meal • *Richard Labonté* • 93
Fell's Meat Loaf • *M.E. Kerr* • 96
Dinner Party Meat Loaf • *Tom Bianchi* • 97
Politically Incorrect Pot Roast • *Pat Califia* • 98

Sweet Climax: Dessert 101

Sinful Red Velvet Cake • *Dorothy Allison* • 103
The Apple Pie That Seduced My Girlfriend • *Rebecca Brown* • 106
The Night the Bowl Sang • *Joan Nestle and Lee Hudson* • 110
Pecan Pie • *Nisa Donnelly* • 114
Ode to Flan • *Barbara Wilson* • 116
Cranberry Walnut Pie • *Steven Saylor* • 120
Linda's Amazing Coconut Pie • *Matthew Rettenmund* • 121
The Trouble with Tippy • *Mabel Maney* • 122
Gingered Poached Pears with Pecan and Raspberry Filling • *Michael Bronski* • 126

Queer Nibbly Bits: Defying Category 129

Noodle Kugel • *Robert Glück* • 131
Aloo Ghobi • *Surina Kahn* • 132
Potato Latkes • *Karen X. Tulchinsky* • 134
Coleslaw for the Queen • *Tanya Huff* • 137
Old-Time Favorites • *Kevin Killian* • 140
Fab Frito ReciPie • *D. Travers Scott* • 142
Vegetarian-Chili Frito Pie • *Tristan Taormino* • 144
I Love Lucy Dog Biscuits for Your Beloved Pet • *Louise Rafkin* • 146
Painted Lady Peppers • *Deb Price and Joyce Murdoch* • 148
Adventures in Innovation: or It's Nouvelle, But Is It Cuisine? • *Geoff Ryman* • 149

About the Editor • 155
Appendix: Beneficiary Organizations • 157
Index • 163

Introduction

One of the most important revelations I've had about cooking happened in the glorious kitchen of my editor, Frédérique Delacoste—part of which is featured on the front cover of this book—as we were sitting at the table discussing plans for this project. She said, off-handedly, that the most important aspect of cooking was never to let the food know you're afraid of it.

While this may seem simplistic or trite, it was a true epiphany for me. I've never been an adventurous cook or eater, and in large part this is because I'm afraid of foods I'm not familiar with, and of my general ignorance of how to prepare foods. Ironically, I've been cooking for myself for over a decade now, usually very simple foods that require a minimum of supervision and preparation. Her cavalier aphorism gave me a mantra to latch onto as I confronted my entire philosophy toward food, since compiling this cookbook has been, in many ways, a baptism by fire for me.

This book evolved, in large part, out of my sense of frustration at the way a body—anybody, my body—can and does grow used to anything, even constant death and dying. As so many of us have, I've watched friends, editors, professors die in quick succession, people I have known personally and who have had a profound influence on me. And it was in many ways expected. Born in 1971, I have grown up in the shadow of the epidemic. AIDS has been a constant specter on my consciousness; I cannot remember a time before AIDS. But at the same time it remains distant, or I distance it, reducing AIDS to icons such as red ribbons—an important acknowledgment, but in many ways a dehumanizing one. Even as people I knew (and so many others) were fighting and dying from the disease, it was hard to keep a human focus amidst talk of statistics and politics, protease inhibitors and viral load. Or perhaps it was simply too easy to adopt the Manhattanite creed of "don't look, don't get involved" as I hurried through my life, self-involved.

I was frustrated with myself for not doing something to fight the disease, frustrated at the way I could not manage to maintain anger and outrage, at government inaction and homophobia and countless other villains, abstract or concrete. In many ways, my generation of Stonewall babies, as a generation, seems to be missing the same sort of anger that spawned ACT UP and Queer Nation, in large part because we've inherited a more comfortable world than they faced, thanks to gains they earned for us. Which is not to say that ACT UP and Queer Nation and my generation of Stonewall babies are not angry and fighting still; they are. And they have won and are winning victories, which should be celebrated, but which are not sufficient. It is too easy, and too tempting, to settle on the gains we've won, and leave other battles for other people to fight. Anger is such a difficult emotion to live with, especially over time. It is an unrewarding emotion, raw and caustic—and tremendously powerful. I think we need a healthy dose of new anger now, for we are not out of this crisis by a long shot, and won't be until a cure is found and the dying stops. And even then, we will be mourning for so many.

This project, then, is my way of doing something with my anger and frustration. It happened as a book because that's what I know how to make. Writing, rather than cooking, is my method of influencing the world.

Too many cooks, it is said, will spoil the stew. *Food for Life,* however, is not intended to be a meal on its own; this book has a larger vision, a menu that aims to encompass and to nourish a community. It draws on the vast cross-section of the lesbian and gay community—actors, activists, athletes, musicians, writers, and others—queers from all walks of life, donating their favorite recipes and their thoughts on food. It is a project that I hope will result in a renewed sense of activism, of concern and care-giving.

All royalties generated from the sale of this book will be donated to regional organizations that provide food to homebound people with AIDS. These organizations, listed in the Appendix, serve over ten thousand meals each day, and are a fraction of the organizations, soup kitchens and individuals who provide food to people infected with HIV and their families. Such organizations rely heavily on the contributions of individual donors, and especially on the people who volunteer their time and energy, their spirit and humanity, to care for others. There is really nothing that can compare with the intimacy of the physical, the directness and power of human-to-human contact.

Food and eating are some of the most primal ways people interact with each other, and sharing meals with someone, especially someone who is ill, can be a wonderful and heartening experience for both parties. As Nisa Donnelly says in the anecdote accompanying her Pecan Pie recipe: "It cannot replace T-cells or cure lesions or rebuild immune systems, I know that, too. It is only pie, after all, not magic. Except for that moment, that first long glorious moment, when it tastes a great deal like love."

The recipes and anecdotes in this book strive to be as human as possible. They are personal, often comic, glimpses into the lives of lesbian and gay celebrities and public figures. They share foibles and successes, memories of childhood and family. Some recount culinary seductions. They are meant to entertain, to arouse hunger and other passions, to titillate and amuse, to inspire.

Cook them in good health. And enjoy the many long glorious moments when they taste a great deal like love.

Lawrence Schimel
August 1996

10

Organization

The organization of a cookbook is a lot less intuitive than it first seems. I had to force some semblance of order on the diverse recipes that were contributed to this project, and not everything fit exactly. However, one of the secrets to cooking, I've learned, is flexibility, an openness to try something new, a spirit of adventure. (And a willingness to accept that not all cooking will result in culinary masterpieces and that even dishes you've cooked successfully in the past may not turn out the same way again.) Because this cookbook was never intended to be a guide to a particular sort of cuisine, many of the recipes will need to be complemented with other dishes whose recipes you'll have to get from parents, friends, or other cookbooks.

Certain sections contain more recipes than others—it looks like our community has quite a sweet tooth, or at least that many of us find baking a relaxing and enjoyable pasttime. Certain recipes may've gone into other sections, but I felt, for the balance of the book, a need to beef up the section where they appear.

This cookbook is designed, in many ways, to be a delectable reading experience in addition to being functional. So, enjoy both the reading and the eating, and if you're anything like me, don't feel daunted by the sheer number and diversity of recipes herein: only the most versatile of cooks—and eaters—will try every dish in this collection.

Nutrition and HIV

While some of these recipes are health-conscious, others throw nutritional concerns to the wind. Although this cookbook is not intended to provide a meal regimen for persons infected with HIV, this does not mean that the recipes herein cannot be eaten and enjoyed by HIV-positive people. In fact, many of the recipes, especially the desserts, might be especially helpful for people trying to avoid losing weight. One of the most important nutritional goals for a person with HIV is to maintain body weight and muscles. Foods that are otherwise taboo in a healthy diet may provide an important source of calories. Even if you're HIV-positive and asymptomatic, it might be helpful to try and put on a few extra pounds.

I urge anyone who is HIV-positive to speak with a registered dietician (R.D.) or physician (M.D.) about weight-maintenance strategies. For more information, you can contact Nutritionists In AIDS Care (NIAC) at (212) 439-8073.

Another resource is the book *Dr. David Reuben's Quick Weight-Gain Program* (Crown). Yes, this is the same Dr. Reuben who wrote *Everything You Always Wanted to Know about Sex but Were Afraid to Ask* with its unenlightened and negative views of homosexuality. Necessity sometimes makes strange bedfellows. This is the only commercial book on the subject of weight gain of which I'm aware, and it does contain much useful information and strategies for people combating unwanted and unexpected weight loss.

Also of interest is *The Immune Support Cookbook* by Mary Hale and Chris Miller (Birch Lane Press), which prescribes a meal regimen of foods that may help bolster the body's immune system.

Getting Wet:

Soups

SOUPS ARE OFTEN CONSIDERED A STARTER COURSE, a culinary foreplay as it were, which is why the cookbook begins here. They can, of course, also be a meal in and of themselves.

Perhaps it's global warming, but New York winters have been growing worse than ever, so I try to keep a soup pot going at all times. A vegetable stew can recover from pretty much any vegetable you add to it. I once tried to cook a pea soup without knowing that I had to presoak the dried legumes overnight. It took days for the peas to reduce, so I made matzo balls and cooked them in the broth at the top of the pot; by the time I'd eaten all of them, the peas had reduced—a two-tier soup.

Another reason I love soups: my lentil soup is the one thing I've ever made that my mother has vocally approved of—no small potatoes for any child, especially a budding Jewish mother.

In addition to the recipes in this section, you'll find Dilled Pea Soup in the next section, as an accompaniment to Marion Dane Bauer's Johnny Cake recipe.

Until then, may your appetites be whetted by these special broths and stews.

L.S.

Paul Russell

PHOTO: DIXIE SHERIDAN

*T*his recipe comes from my futile attempts to duplicate a fine red lentil soup I encountered often during my travels in Turkey. I remember two dark and beautiful boys, perhaps brothers, spooning such soup avidly into their mouths in a bus-station restaurant in the holy city of Konya. Who they were, what had brought them there, where they were going, why they were so impressively, even rapturously hungry: those are mysteries, as is some essential ingredient— perhaps culinary, perhaps merely atmospheric—that continues to elude me in my quest to recover the exact taste of that Turkish soup. Nevertheless, I have found that this version is not unpleasing.

Turkish Red Lentil Soup

2 small onions, finely chopped
1 tablespoon olive oil
6 cups chicken stock
1 ½ cups dried red (Egyptian) lentils (available from most organic or health food stores)
1 carrot, shredded
3 teaspoons cumin
1 egg yolk (optional)
3 tablespoons milk (optional)
Salt and pepper to taste

In the bottom of a large pot, sauté the chopped onions in olive oil until golden. Add the chicken stock, dried red lentils, and shredded carrot. Bring to a boil; then simmer, covered, for 1¼ hours.

Add the cumin (not too early, or a bitter taste will result). Simmer another 5 to 10 minutes, until the red lentils are more or less completely dissolved. For a heartier version, add 1 egg yolk and 3 tablespoons of milk at this point.

Season to taste with salt and pepper. The Turks often squeeze in a bit of lemon juice as a final touch. Serves four.

PAUL RUSSELL is a novelist whose works include *The Salt Point, Sea of Tranquillity,* and *Boys of Life.* He teaches at Vassar College.

Patricia Nell Warren

*W*here food is concerned, nothing is more magical than things that I grow myself.

Partly it's an old ranch thing—I grew up watering and weeding a vast World War II "victory garden" that fed a whole ranch—family and hired men. Partly it's a gay thing. Over the years, I have pondered on the love that so many gay people feel for good eating, and for making a piece of earth beautiful and fruitful. Maybe the social agony that we experience has left many of us feeling cut off from the rest of Life. So we make a super-human effort to get back in touch with the roots of existence, which is not only our sense of self, but the Earth Herself. We can do this with food, gardening and a closeness with the Land. In my novel The Front Runner, *when coach Harlan Brown and runner Billy Sive move into a house together, they take possession of the yard as well—and plant a garden.*

Home-grown food is far better-tasting and less chemically polluted than com-mercial food. My Native American relatives always had gardens, even the poor ones on the reservation, who had to eat prairie dogs to stay alive during lean times. Some of the most wonderful stories that they shared with me were about food (including a hundred ways to cook prairie dog).

Dream Soup is a kind of soup/stew that some Western tribes call posole *(pronounced po-so-lay). You can vary it to what's in the garden, on the shelf, in the fridge or freezer.*

Corn is the key ingredient of posole—its very spirit. To say corn *in the many native languages of the Peoples is to say* mother, *because its young juice is like milk. Most Americans eat corn in the baby stage, so they don't have a clue how* tasty corn is when it goes adult and starchy on the ear, yet still soft enough to cook in an hour or so. I remember visiting a friend in the Santo Domingo pueblo on the Rio Grande in the early 1980s, during the Corn Dances. All of us were eating mature boiled corn, with posole on the side, till we almost burst. Little kids wandered around carrying an ear of corn, gnawing it. It was their answer to the candy bar. Truly we have lost the ability to enjoy the essence of corn, without butter or other white-man frills.

To be stored indefinitely, corn must be dried hard, like beans. To cook it, you have to soak it overnight, just like beans, and cook it till tender. This "parched corn" (as the anthros call it) is what kept native Americans alive for 5000 years. Treated with lye water, corn turns to hominy.

Since those One Is the Sun years, I always try to grow some corn wherever I live, and carry with me a few dried ears of Golden Bantam for seed. Golden Bantam is a short compact plant with small ears, an old variety that's been around for centuries. It is a beautiful and ornamental plant in a suburban flower bed if that's the only place you've got to grow things. And it matures fast—75 days. Plant a few seeds once a week from last frost till mid-July for waves of one corn feast a week through the season. Corn likes sun and rich soil and adequate water. It grows well in wild riotous pagan intermixings with other plants, like squash and beans and tomatoes.

Meat is numero dos in posole, but gives it body. When I was visiting a medicine chief and his family on the Navajo reservation in the 1980s, while I was writing One Is the Sun, they fed me posole made with desert-bred mutton, served up with a platter of smoking hot fry bread. But you can make posole with beef, pork, lamb, venison, poultry, whatever meat you fancy.

My métis (mixed blood) relatives from Montana taught me how to make posole with pheasant meat. One cousin always kept a penful of home-raised pheasants on his little ranch on the Crow reservation. Pheasant is wonderful eating—the lowest-fat and highest-protein of poultry meats. Americans are missing something when they relegate this bird to holiday and high-end eating. Once you are hooked on free-range pheasant, the very taste of factory chicken will turn your stomach! In the late 1980s, when I had an organic poultry farm in northern California to support myself during a lean time on One Is the Sun, I raised my own pheasant and made "many plenty" posoles. (My cousin always accompanied these words "many plenty" with his expressive brown hands carving the appropriate sign-language sign in the air).

Herbs are important. The old people added whatever herbs were around, so there is no fixed list. Put in the ones you like. Dried or fresh is okay.

Surprise—there is no onion in posole. I asked one of my Indian aunties why. She said that the old-time cooks didn't always use onions. "You can get the taste of the meat and all those other things a lot better," she said, "if you don't smother it in onion."

This is one of those recipes where there are no fixed ingredients. Your imagination and knowledge of your own personal and subtle tastes are challenged. It's also a dish that gets better with re-heating.

It may seem like a long way from the Hopi corn gardens to Santa Monica Boulevard, but really it's not so far. Think of all the people in the gay community who are mixed bloods like me! Berkeley sociologist and native activist Jack Forbes estimated that millions of Americans have significant traces of native blood. It is a mostly unacknowledged, yet potent, thread that runs through many of us—the ancestry of many rich cultures and great Peoples where gay people were more accepted than in the U.S. today.

As I write this, I am moving to a new home in Los Angeles and plan a small but intensive raised garden alongside of the parking area. It measures only about five feet by thirty feet but will grow many plenty things to eat. Along the back, tomatoes and beans will crawl up the board fence. Along the front, ground-hugging herbs and lettuces will spill over the border. In the middle—the corn. An ear of Golden Bantam will get shelled and planted, the first wave of corn will grow—and I'll share the bounty of fifteen or twenty ears with my friends.

PATRICIA NELL WARREN is author of the best-selling novel and cult classic *The Front Runner*, among many other novels, short stories, articles, and poems. Her current publisher is Wildcat Press.

Dream Soup

Equal amounts of the following: your favorite meat, cubed potatoes, diced tomatoes and cut corn (or hominy)

Fresh or dried herbs (Thyme is a good one.)

Several cubes of good quality beef extract

Spring water

Sea salt

Pepper

Hot peppers—jalapeños or whatever you've got (optional)

Lightly brown the meat in a heavy skillet without fat, moving it with a fork to keep it from burning. Layer the meat in a kettle alternately with the potatoes, tomatoes and corn. Sprinkle the herbs, spices, salt and beef cubes over the top. Add water till it barely covers the kettle contents and spices. Boil out the skillet and add the carbonized juices to the pot.

Bring slowly to a simmer, cover and simmer over low heat till the meat and corn is tender. DO NOT STIR. This keeps the pieces of meat and vegetable intact. The spices will simmer slowly down to the bottom of the kettle.

Serve in large bowls with big soup spoons and your favorite hot bread on the side.

Note: If you are going all the way, and using dried corn, soak it and simmer it separately till close to done, before combining it with the posole.

Cecilia Tan

*F*ood is about family and the rituals and traditions of eating together. One Tan family tradition that my mother started when I was younger was to make Peking Duck on Thanksgiving instead of turkey. Duck is much tastier, and creates much less in the way of leftovers no one wants to eat. To make Peking Duck right, you have to parboil the ducks and then let them hang up for a day to let the blood run out and dry out the skin. My mother had hung the duck in the basement when the gas man came to read the meter. She wondered why he came upstairs with such a strange expression on his face. I guess people are really not prepared to see a duck carcass hanging around the house.

Now that I've been out of my parents' house for several years, I have my own chosen family over for Thanksgiving. One year we hung the ducks in the stair-well to the basement and one of our housemates hit his head on them. Our most recent attempt involved commandeering the first-floor bathroom and a precari-ous kludge made of a camera tripod, a broom handle, and twine...and keeping the cat out.

This is a recipe I made up when trying to recreate a Filipino dish called arroz caldo (rice stew) and had only a vague idea of how to go about it. The result is a gingery rice porridge that is very good for cold days!

CECILIA TAN is the publisher and editor of Circlet Press. Her own writings have appeared in numerous anthologies, including *Dark Angels* and *Switch Hitters*, and in periodicals ranging from *Penthouse* to *Ms*. She lives in Boston.

Chicken Rice Stew

3 cups cooked rice
3 stalks celery
2 onions
10 cloves garlic, peeled
¾ pound diced chicken breast
   or thigh
5 cups chicken broth
6 slices ginger (1-inch
   diameter, ⅛-inch thick)
2 tablespoons frying oil
Salt and pepper
Soy sauce (optional)

This takes 45 minutes to prepare if you have a rice cooker or have pre-cooked/left-over rice. Start the rice in the rice cooker. While it is cooking, slice the celery cross-wise into very thin crescents, mince the onion, and slice the garlic into slivers. Dice the chicken.

Heat the chicken stock in a large pot (a 5-quart Dutch oven or larger) with half of the garlic and ginger. In a wok, or a large frying pan, stir fry the remaining garlic, ginger, onions, and celery until the onions are translucent and the celery is soft. Set the vegetables aside.

Pat the diced chicken dry with paper towels and toss in a bowl with 2 to 3 tablespoons of cornstarch. Once the chicken is coated and dry to the touch, heat the oil in the wok or pan and stir fry until the meat is solid white on all sides, with a bit browned. The cornstarch affects the heat transfer into the meat so it comes out extremely soft—it is served in Chinese restaurants as a stir-fry dish called "Velvet Chicken" because of the texture.

As soon as the chicken is done, add it and the vegetables to the heated stock and stir. Then add the cooked rice. Cover and simmer for 10 to 20 minutes. Add salt, or soy sauce, and pepper to taste.

If you cook this longer, until the liquid is absorbed by the rice, you get something very similar to arroz con pollo, a kind of Hispanic chicken-and-rice pilaf. If you add more broth, a touch of lime juice, and fresh cilantro, you have something very similar to the Vietnamese rice chowder called chao. If you don't like crunching down on the slivers of ginger, grate it instead of slicing it.

Gavin Geoffrey Dillard

This is one of the healthiest ways to eat vegetables, for the short cooking time, and keeps well in the fridge. Winter squash are the most nutritious—butternuts my personal fave—though a good pumpkin variation with an additional shot of cinnamon gives good Thanksgiving.

There are rumors that cumin arrests HIV, among other wonders (shhh! don't tell the AMA, let them sleep...). I have doubled the amount used for this recipe 'cause I love the stuff. This soup (roughly 40 calories per serving) and brown rice could sustain a person indefinitely. Use chemical-free chicken broth (nix on Swanson's) and omit the dairy if it makes you snotty like it does most people....

GAVIN GEOFFREY DILLARD is a poet whose books include *Pagan Love Songs, Naked Poet,* and *Yellow Snow.* He lives in Northern California.

Swami Shankara's Squash and Cumin Soup, Hot or Cold

1 ½ pounds squash
   (4 medium crookneck,
   2 medium butternut, 4-ish
   acorns, etc.), trimmed and
   diced
1 medium carrot, sliced
1 large onion, chopped
1 leek (white part, sliced) or
   several shallots
2 (or more) cloves garlic
3 cups chicken broth,
   vegetable stock, or 3 cups
   water with 4 boullion
   cubes
1 teaspoon ground cumin
⅛ teaspoon nutmeg
   (optional) or ½ teaspoon
   turmeric (good color)
½ teaspoon salt (optional)
A dash of Tabasco (optional)
A pinch of cayenne (optional)
¼ cup plain yogurt or sour
   cream (optional)
Chopped chives, parsley or
   cilantro (optional)

In a large saucepan, place the vegetables, stock, cumin, and nutmeg. Cover and simmer for 15 to 20 minutes.

Add salt, Tabasco, cayenne (or an additional raw clove of garlic) and whoosh it all in a blender or food processor. Chill for a summer soup, or serve hot in winter with that dollop of yogurt or sour cream and chopped chives, parsley, or cilantro. Serves six small queens, or two really big and hairy ones.

Lesléa Newman

Grandma Ruthie's Chicken Soup for Very Special People

A nice chicken
5 fat carrots
1 bunch celery
Fresh dill
Fresh parsley
A bissl salt, if desired

Put the chicken into a soup pot, preferably one used for many years by your mother or grandmother. Peel the carrots, cut them into hunks the size of Lincoln Logs and throw them into the pot. Cut the celery (including leaves) into inch-long slices and throw them in, too. Chop the dill and parsley and add them to the pot. Add salt if desired. How much? Enough. Fill the whole thing with enough water to cover the contents, put the lid on the pot and set it on the stove. When the soup boils, tilt the lid so a little steam can escape. Let it simmer for 1 1/2 hours, or until the chicken is so tender it falls off the bones.

Take the chicken out of the pot (carefully so you don't burn yourself) and remove the chicken meat from the bones. Cut it into bite-size pieces and put them back in the pot.

Grandma Ruthie's Matzo Balls

1/2 cup matzo meal
2 eggs
2 tablespoons broth
2 tablespoons oil

While the soup is cooking, set another soup pot of water up to boil. Mix ingredients together. Cover and refrigerate for 20 minutes.

Wash your hands well, remove your rings, and take the mix from the refrigerator. Roll into balls about 1 inch diameter and drop them into the boiling water. (If hands get sticky, dip them in a bowl of ice-cold water.) Cover the matzo balls tightly and let them boil for 20 minutes.

Add them to the chicken soup, and serve it to someone you love with challa, Manishevitz wine and homemade applesauce (latkes or blintzes wouldn't be bad either, but that's another story).

LESLÉA NEWMAN is perhaps best-known for her children's books, *Heather Has Two Mommies* and *Gloria Goes to Gay Pride*, which have been frequent targets of censorship and the focus of many controversies in education and libraries. She is also the author or editor of many titles for adults, including *The Femme Mystique, My Lover Is a Woman, A Letter to Harvey Milk*, and *Out of the Closet and Nothing to Wear*.

Everything That Rises:

A Baker's Half Dozen

I NO LONGER HAVE THE PATIENCE TO BAKE. When I was younger, I invented all sorts of breads, many of which resembled matzos or pones because, aside from a few science experiments with yeast, I didn't have the patience to allow dough to rise properly. I was able to pound all the air bubbles out of a slab of clay, but quickly lost interest when it came to kneading dough, which I instead formed into clay-like figurines and pots. At least I was religious about eating all the evidence from these experiments, because I do love fresh-baked bread and was willing to forgive my own mistakes to have some.

The summer I lived in Granada, Spain, I exulted in the kiosks on each corner that sold fresh baguettes, in addition to magazines and sodas, which is all that's offered at the kiosks on New York street corners. Fortunately, some excellent bakers have booths at the local green market.

However, sometimes you've a yen to bake your own bread. It's a wonderful feeling, to eat bread you've baked yourself, and can be a relaxing, cathartic experience (I'm told), a way to massage the day's stresses away on a lump of dough.

With the help of these recipes, you'll be able to avoid my teenage mishaps, and rise to the occasion of baking.

L.S.

RuPaul

This is the equivalent of pan-fried cornbread but it's served like hot cereal. To this day, my sisters and I make it when we're together. It's the ultimate in comfort food.

Breakfast Cush Cush

6 cups water
½ teaspoon salt
1 ½ cups yellow cornmeal
1 teaspoon Crisco shortening
1 cup milk, heated
2 tablespoons sugar
1 tablespoon butter

Bring the water and salt to boil in a medium saucepan. Reduce the heat and stir in the cornmeal. Cook over low heat, stirring constantly, until thick, about 15 minutes.

Melt the shortening in a large nonstick skillet, spoon the cornmeal mixture into the skillet. Cook until lightly browned, stirring 2 to 3 minutes.

Place Cush Cush into serving bowls; top with heated milk, sugar, and butter; mix well and eat.

Recording artist, entertainer, and drag queen, **RUPAUL** is the Chairperson for the MAC AIDS Fund and the Momentum Project in New York City. His autobiography, *Lettin' It All Hang Out*, has recently been published by Hyperion.

Marion Dane Bauer

*W*hen the first frost of autumn ends the harvest, Ann and I grieve over the loss of the fresh vegetables we have been buying from a nearby farmer's market all summer long. Here in Minnesota, the growing season is always too short. But then we also turn back, with renewed enthusiasm, to our usual winter fare of thick homemade soups and breads of all kinds.

This cornbread recipe came from my Minnesota-farm-born mother. (A friend from the South insists that we Northerners know nothing of true cornbread, but the Johnny Cake I grew up with is as true for me as her version is for her.)

MARION DANE BAUER is the author of thirteen books for young readers, including *On My Honor*, a Newbery Honor book, and *A Question of Trust*. She is also editor of *Am I Blue?: Coming Out from the Silence*, an anthology of stories with lesbian and gay themes for young adults.

Johnny Cake

2 cups coarse yellow cornmeal
1 cup flour
1 ½ teaspoons baking powder
½ teaspoon baking soda
½ teaspoon salt
1 large egg, or 2 small
⅓ cup melted bacon fat or
    vegetable oil
1 ½ cups buttermilk

Mix dry ingredients. Beat in the egg, fat, and buttermilk. (I substitute vegetable oil for the melted bacon fat, and, in fact, my mother does, too, these days.) Pour into a well-greased oblong pan or muffin tins. Bake at 375 degrees for about 35 minutes.

I like the Johnny Cake best split and crisped in the oven after the first day. If you want to try this, bake the thinly cut pieces again until they are thoroughly dry. In this form, they can be saved in a plastic bag for many days.

And with the cornbread one must, of course, have a hearty vegetable soup.

Dilled Pea Soup

2 cups dried green split peas
1 tablespoon olive oil
1 large onion, chopped
2 cloves garlic, minced
1 cup chopped carrots
1 cup chopped celery
Chicken or vegetable broth
2 tablespoons tamari soy
    sauce
¼ teaspoon black pepper
½ cup snipped fresh dill
2 ½ cups cubed potatoes

Presoak the peas and pour off the water.

Sauté the onion, garlic, carrots, and celery in the oil. Add the other ingredients to the peas with enough broth to cover. Cook until the peas are very soft and the potatoes are done. Add broth as needed. Serve with Johnny Cake fresh from the oven or crisped. And enjoy!

Jewelle Gomez

In 1986, when poet Cheryl Clarke and I moved in together, we discovered we had two more things in common: our cast-iron frying pans and our family recipes for cornbread. That year we were invited to a winter solstice celebration and were asked to bring a family dish and talk about our ethnic or cultural relationship to it. Cheryl made cornbread and explained that she was no longer certain which one of the iron skillets belonged to her mother and which had belonged to my great-grandmother.

Because my great-grandmother, Grace, had to eat corn every day as a child on an Iowa Indian reservation, she didn't like to eat cornbread. But my stepmother, Henrietta, a Boston chef (by way of Gulfport, Mississippi) made cornbread her specialty. When we were with her, I always got Grace to take a bite, just for luck. For me it represents the maize that fed the Native

30

American people and animals of the American plains, and the African-American ability to adapt and thrive in this country. For both Cheryl and I, it was the delicate and hardy food that said who we are.

A decade later, Cheryl and I live on opposite sides of the country; when we get together the memories are bittersweet, and cornbread is still a coarse joy, full of history, full of dreams.

Cornbread

1 cup yellow cornmeal
1 tablespoon baking powder
1 cup unbleached white flour
½ teaspoon salt
1 egg
¼ cup corn oil
1 cup milk, plain or sweet
1 eleven-ounce can whole-kernel corn (without liquid), or 1 medium onion

Mix the cornmeal, baking powder, flour, and salt. Add the egg, oil, and milk. Begin to blend, then add the kernel corn. The mixture remains thick and grainy. Make sure that all the cornmeal is blended in.

Coat the bottom and sides of a 9-inch iron skillet with corn oil and pour the batter into it. Place it on a rack in the center of the oven, and bake at 400 degrees for 25 minutes.

Touch the center: if firm, it's done. Or you can kind of thump it lightly in the center and it should sound hollow. The top should be golden brown around the edges. You can also substitute diced onions for the kernel corn.

Serve with butter, jam, or (my favorite) Vermont maple syrup.

JEWELLE GOMEZ is the author of numerous works of fiction, essays, and poetry, including *The Gilda Stories*, winner of the Lambda Literary Award, *Forty-Three Septembers*, *Oral Tradition*, and *Flamingoes and Bears*, among others. She lives in San Francisco.

Stephanie Rosenbaum

It's the non-baker's night-mare: ten fussy people coming to brunch, and not one of them likes Pop-Tarts! Even if your idea of baking is popping a frozen bagel in the microwave, don't be daunted: these scones will not let you down. To ensure a light and flaky result, don't pummel the dough. Handle it just enough to make your ingredients stick together, and your delicacy will be rewarded. At the risk of sounding like the lesbian Martha Stewart, this recipe is a great way to put all those whimsically shaped biscuit cutters to use. (You do have a collection of antique biscuit cutters, don't you?) So festive! So amusing! For a recent femmes-only bridal shower, I cut out all the scones (as well as the cookies and the tea sandwiches—it's easy to get carried away) with a variety of heart-shaped cutters. You can also use a knife and cut out your own shapes, or just divide the dough into triangular wedges. The egg-yolk wash is optional, but it does give the finished product a very shiny and appealing crust.

Tea-Time Scones

3 cups all-purpose flour
⅓ cup sugar
2 ½ teaspoons baking powder
½ teaspoon baking soda
½ teaspoon salt
½ cup cold butter (1 stick)
½ to ¾ cup buttermilk
½ cup currants
½ cup golden raisins

Glaze: 1 egg yolk mixed with
1 tablespoon cold water

Preheat oven to 375 degrees.

Sift together the flour, sugar, baking powder, baking soda, and salt. Cut butter into chunks and combine with dry ingredients using a pastry blender or your fingertips. Rub the mixture until it resembles dry oatmeal, with a few bigger flakes. Using a fork, toss in the buttermilk a little at a time, just enough to get a soft, workable dough—don't let the mixture get too wet. Mix in the currants and raisins.

Turn the dough out onto a lightly floured surface and knead gently 3 or 4 times to form a smooth, pliable dough. Pat the dough into a circle approximately ¾ inch thick. Cut out scones using a biscuit cutter or the rim of a small glass. Place the scones on a greased cookie sheet and glaze, using a pastry brush or the back of a spoon. Bake 15 to 20 minutes until golden brown. Best served warm, with butter and jam.

STEPHANIE ROSENBAUM writes weekly restaurant reviews for the *San Francisco Bay Guardian*, as well as a monthly pastry column called "Queen of Tarts." She also writes about fashion, the arts, and lifestyle issues for numerous local and national publications, including *Out*, *Vegetarian Times*, *Fad*, *Bay Area Reporter*, and the *Bay Times*.

Photo: Robert Pruzan

Thom Gunn

This is so easy that you can make it even if you think you are too macho to cook. It is from Catalonia, and would be perfect to attract that Catalan highway patrolman you have been after for so long.

Tomato Bread

French bread
Olive oil
Tomato
Salt

Take a slice of French bread (bâtard not baguette), brush it with olive oil and put it in the oven until it is toasted a bit. Then cut open a ripe tomato, and rub half of it over the slice. Keep the ruined half-tomato for a spaghetti sauce the next day, and serve the Tomato Bread on the toe of one of your boots. Balance with a line of your favorite aphrodisiac on your other boot-toe, and you have Felipe just where you want him.

Sprinkle a bit of salt on the Tomato Bread, if you can manage it.

THOM GUNN'S *Collected Poems* were recently published by Farrar, Straus & Giroux. He is the author of eleven previous collections, including *The Man with Night Sweats, My Sad Captains, Moly, The Passages of Joy, Jack Straw's Castle,* and others. Born in England, he's made his home in San Francisco since 1954.

Drag for Food:

Dressings and Marinades

I WAS SHOCKED the day my friend Royal Fraser came over for lunch and made us a delicious, intriguing salad dressing in less than a minute. That morning I'd dashed out to the local farmer's market for fresh greens and melon, a light midday meal during an oppressive summer day. I didn't, however, have any salad dressing in the fridge; it's something I'm unaccustomed to using, personally, preferring my greenery plain. Royal poured balsamic vinegar, olive oil, and—this was the shock, for me—some raspberry jam into a bowl and whisked it with a fork. The resultant tangy/sweet dressing has now become a staple in my diet, and one that I've used to impress other friends and dates.

Most of the recipes in this section are versatile, and can be used to spice up salads, sandwiches, meats, "whatever"—to borrow from the philosophy that Aiden Shaw's recipe illustrates. So keep them in mind as you read other sections of this book, and don't be surprised to find ideas or recipes for dressings and marinades in other sections, such as Ellen Kushner's "Everything but the Grill" tucked in with the fish.

Experiment. Be creative. Be flamboyant—this is, after all, drag for food.

L.S.

Martina Navratilova

An old standby!

Pesto

1 cup olive oil
2 cloves garlic, peeled
½ cup fresh basil
1 teaspoon salt
¼ teaspoon pepper
2 tablespoons pine nuts
1 cup parsley
Grated Parmesan cheese

Mix the oil, garlic, and basil at high speed in a blender. Let the contents sit for at least 15 minutes. Then add the salt, pepper, and pine nuts and mix at low speed. Add the parsley and mix again at low speed. Add the Parmesan cheese—mixing by hand—to desired texture and taste. Serve on pasta or chicken.

MARTINA NAVRATILOVA is the world's most famous tennis player, winner of a record nine Wimbledon Championships. Born in Czechoslovakia, she lives now in Aspen, Colorado.

MARCUS (SITTING ATOP COUNTER), DANIELE AND AIDEN SHAW   PHOTO: JAMES AND JAMES

Aiden Shaw

Whatever

This is not so much a recipe as a kitchen philosophy, or a food-related lifestyle. Firstly, this recipe has to involve two or three people. Any more gets crowded in my small kitchen, and conversation tends to waver into showing off and competition; it seems to lose its intimacy. The friends in this recipe are Daniele and Marcus, two of my dearest. They are both vegetarians, whereas I eat fish, so this follows their dietary guidelines. Having very busy lives and taking into account my alterable blood-sugar level, this has got to be a fast, easy-to-prepare meal. We believe that if food is prepared with love, it leads to happy-tummy.

AIDEN SHAW is the author of a novel, *Brutal*, among other works of fiction and poetry. A popular performer in erotic videos, he is also the singer in the band Whatever. He lives in London.

There are some basic ingredients that have to be in the house:

A-list:
Fresh garlic
Fresh ginger
Some kind of citrus fruit,
    preferably lime
Honey

B-list:
Miso
Soy sauce
Your favorite spices (caraway,
    aniseed, Chinese five-spice)

These last a long time, so they can always be kept on hand and used in various combinations. The basic idea behind this treat is that "whatever" is in the kitchen can be used as long as you add the above magic ingredients.

The Whatever Soup

Add whatever vegetables, impulses, etc. Boil up and add the garlic, ginger, and lime. Adding your favorite spices and miso make it a winter special.

The Whatever Salad Dressing

Add whatever vegetables, fruits, nuts, etc. "Chop and mix" (registered trademark) and add a dressing of garlic, ginger, lime, and honey. Sweet, light, and summery.

The Whatever Tortilla

Scramble some free-range eggs (I use just the whites) and pour into a shallow pan. Add whatever peppers, mushrooms, onions are in the fridge. Add garlic and ginger to make this unusually satisfying and very nutritious any time of the year. (Fresh cilantro makes this a dream.)

So go for it, have fun, and remember anything shared (including shopping) makes for double the fun.

Betty Dodson

Garlic Mud for Self-Lovers

3 heads garlic
Imported raw green olive oil
   from the first pressing
Bernard Jensen's Broth or
   Seasoning
Balsamic vinegar

Get the best olive oil money can buy. My favorite is Carother's Olive Oil. If you order six or more quarts at a time, you can buy wholesale direct from the distributor (810/235-2055). Bernard Jensen's Broth or Seasoning (a powdered vegetable mix) is available in most health food stores, or write to Bernard Jensen Products/PO Box 8/ Solana Beach, CA 92075.

If you're in the mood for a hand-job, mince the heads of garlic, in the nude if your kitchen is warm enough. Or if you've just had an orgasm, and you want to speed up the process, chop the garlic in a mini-chopper. Inhale the exquisite aroma and touch your genitals occasionally with your garlic-drenched fingers to make sure you're paying attention.

Place the minced garlic in a glass jar with a screw-on lid, cover it with olive oil, and let it sit overnight. The garlic sting will be removed while the delicious flavor remains. This jar of garlic in oil has many uses: spooned into salad dressings, used as a marinade, added to soups and sauces.

For my winter-time favorite, Garlic Mud, place 3 to 4 tablespoons of the oil-soaked garlic in a small, sexy bowl. Add Bernard Jensen's Broth or Seasoning until you get a mud-like consistency. Add a few drops of balsamic vinegar to taste. Spoon onto baked sweet potatoes, steamed vegetables, fish, or chicken. A dab can be placed on a lover's clit or dick for spicy oral sex. Enjoy.

P.S. People who complain that I smell like garlic are emotional vampires who believe in "true love and going steady forever." Garlic Mud protects me from them.

BETTY DODSON, often referred to as "The Mother of Masturbation," is one of the pioneers of the sexual liberation movement. Author of the classic manual *Sex for One,* she has also produced numerous videos and travels widely, giving lectures and workshops.

Stephen McCauley

*W*hen I was nineteen, I moved in with a lover. He was thirty-three and macrobiotic. I was addicted to junk food—hamburgers, donuts, Coca-Cola, you name it. This was my first brush with "health food" and I found it confusing—everything tasted vaguely like dirt. Everything was practically uncooked, and nothing was easy to chew. I'd grown up eating green beans that had been cooked in a pressure cooker for half an hour. Was it safe to eat them raw?

For a long time, I resisted my lover's diet. I bought my own fry pan and cooked my own greasy meals. But little by little, I was won over to vegetarianism. The politics of it appealed to me, not the food, not the supposed health benefits. It was good for the planet, bad for big business, flew in the face of conventions of the day. It was a little like smoking pot instead of drinking beer. Or, for that matter, being gay.

I became a reasonably good cook, learned to bake bread, steam brown rice, make a delicious carrot cake without sugar or honey. Of course, we made more or less everything in a wok. Woks were hard to find in those days (we lived in Vermont) and very popular with vegetarians. We bought everything from the food co-op—tofu, organic vegetables, pots of fresh-ground tahini, jars of tamari. We put tamari on everything, which made everything taste more or less the same—like tamari.

Anyway, the relationship began to go sour. I got depressed. I was so young I thought relationships, like refrigerators, were supposed to last forever. I spent more and more time cooking complicated macro meals, but had less and less interest in eating them. Then everything fell apart. For years after, I couldn't look at tamari. I developed an inability to digest tofu. The smell of tahini made me slightly queasy. Every time I met a potential lover with strong culinary opinions, I retreated.

About ten years later, I met a man who was an incredible cook. A lot of things had changed by then, and the whole food issue didn't seem to matter. Besides, he didn't know anything about macrobiotics. It had never crossed his mind that people might actually eat seaweed. He taught me how to roast a chicken, make pie crust, and marinate swordfish for grilling. That relationship went sour, too, but I kept using his recipes.

The best thing I learned from him was how to make salad dressing. It's very simple, and once I got used to making my own, I found those bottles of store-bought sad and depressing. Whenever I make it, I think about my old friend, and I wonder what he's having for dinner.

Fail-Safe Salad Dressing

2 cloves garlic
1 heaping teaspoon prepared mustard
Your choice of dried herbs
Balsamic vinegar
Maple syrup or honey
Extra-virgin olive oil

Find an 8-ounce glass jar with a nice tight lid. Crush the garlic in a garlic press and dump the pulp into the jar. Add the prepared mustard. It helps if it's good quality mustard, but that isn't essential. Just don't use the grainy kind. Take about a teaspoon of dried herbs, crush them in the palm of your hand, and toss them in. Any herb or combination of herbs will do nicely. Now fill the jar about a quarter of the way up with balsamic vinegar. It has to be balsamic. Shake as hard as possible for 30 seconds. Make sure everything's blended and nice and smooth. Now, add a few drops of maple syrup or honey. Fill the jar all the way up with good, extra-virgin olive oil. Make sure it's fragrant oil, the kind you almost want to drink. Now shake again, hard as you can, for a good solid minute. It should be thick and creamy, a pretty, solid color. You're going to love it. You can use it on sandwiches, too, instead of mayonnaise.

STEPHEN MCCAULEY is the best-selling author of three novels, *The Object of My Affection, The Easy Way Out,* and *The Man of the House.* He lives in Boston.

*Gerry Gomez
Pearlberg*

My best friend Stephen once made the memorable observation that Celestial Seasonings teas are the Spanish Fly of the lesbian community. That's certainly been true in my experience, but here's the food dictum I live by: "A well-dressed salad is the precursor to an undressed girl."

You probably already know how to make a salad, and if you're reading this book, you certainly already know how to undress a girl—or boy, or girl/boy, or whatever—but do you know how to dress a salad so that it not only bites, but sizzles? Herewith is the recipe that has not only preceded the seduction of more women than I can count on both latexed hands, but inspired at least one bi-coastal lesbian ménage à trois in the bargain.

GERRY GOMEZ PEARLBERG'S writings have appeared in various anthologies and magazines. She is the editor of two poetry collections, *The Key to Everything: Classic Lesbian Love Poems,* and *The Zenith of Desire: Contemporary Lesbian Poems about Sex* and the forthcoming *Queer Dog: Homo/Pup/Poetry.* She has worked in the HIV/AIDS prevention and advocacy fields since 1985.

on Salad Dressing

garlic
stard

3 teaspoons Grey Poupon
   Dijon mustard
2 tablespoons red wine
   vinegar
Freshly ground black pepper
1 cup olive oil
A handful of pine nuts

Begin by mincing the garlic. Using a fork or wire whisk, combine the garlic, ground mustard seed, Dijon mustard, and red wine vinegar in a glass bowl. Add some freshly ground black pepper.

Slowly drizzle the olive oil into the mixture, while continually whisking. You may want to add a little extra oil if the dressing seems too "sharp" or acidic for your tastes.

Put the dressing aside and prepare your salad.

Seduction Salad

For added color, use carrots, red cabbage, radicchio, peppers (red, green, yellow), and tomato (red and yellow). Also, experiment with the many wonderful lettuces and greens out there—watercress, endive, red-leaf, mesclun and frisée, to name just a few. After rinsing the lettuce, be sure to use a lettuce drier, air dry, or pat leaves dry with a towel, as an oil-based salad dressing will not adhere properly to watery leaves.

A brief digression on the subject of dulse. I love to include this wonderful sea vegetable in my salads because of its beautiful deep red coloring, its chewy texture, its oceanic sea-goddess origins, and the fact that it contributes a nice salinity to the dish. Like lesbians themselves, packaged dulse is widely available in health food stores and food co-ops. Tear off a few bite-sized pieces, rinse with water, and add it (the sea vegetable, not the lesbian) to the salad. Keep in mind that the less you rinse, the saltier it'll taste—I don't rinse mine off at all, in fact, though the directions on the package suggest doing so. On occasion, tiny snail shells, barnacles, and other minuscule "gifts of the sea" will remain attached to the dulse leaves that they once called home, so at the very least inspect the stuff carefully before tossing it into the salad. I personally get a big kick out of finding these little critters—it gives the salad-preparation experience a very "whole earth" ambiance, and adds an element of environmental surprise to the dining process.

Okay, so now you have your salad, your dulse, your sense of being in touch with Mother Earth, and your dressing. The only thing left to do is toast the pine nuts—which provide the aforementioned "sizzle effect" in this dish.

The pine nuts can be prepared in one of two ways: either by toasting them on a tray in a toaster oven set to "low" or by heating them on the stove in an unoiled pan over a low-medium flame. Whichever method you choose, keep a very close eye on the nuts to prevent them from burning. Pine nuts go from white to brownish (which is how you want them) to burnt-to-a-crisp (which is not how you want them) within a matter of seconds. If you put them in the toaster oven, watch 'em like a hawk, and remove a moment or two before they seem completely browned—they'll continue browning a bit even after removed from the heat. If you cook them on the stove, shake the pan continually to keep the nuts from sticking, until they are tawny-colored.

As you are bringing the pine nuts down the homestretch, dress and toss the salad. As soon as the pine nuts are done, throw them in—the hot nuts should provide a nice sizzle when they make contact with the cool salad. Re-toss well, add a bit more ground pepper to taste, serve, and enjoy.

The Naked
and the Noodle:

(Ad) Dressing Pasta

THE TRICK TO COOKING PASTA can be summed up in one word: accessorize. While pasta comes in many different shapes, thicknesses, and even flavors, what keeps it interesting and varied is the way it's dressed up: the sauce or cheese(s) that accompany it.

I enjoy giving dinner parties, especially if I can do so at someone else's house. It was only when my friend Eve Tetzlaff moved to Moscow for a few years that I inherited a dining-room table, which allowed me to even consider the possibility of entertaining in my own home. But there's something I find exciting about using someone else's kitchen and apartment, especially those that are set up well for cooking and entertaining. Preparations and cleaning, which I find onerous in my own apartment, violating some unspoken tenet of my bachelorhood, I willingly plunge into when using someone else's apartment.

My friend Reg Flowers is an actor who, when he's not on tour, can often be found house-sitting for various actors while they're performing out of town. Shortly after we both graduated from Yale and before he left for a year and a half stint in *Angels in America*, I stayed with him for a few weeks while he was house-sitting in New Haven for one of his professors. It was a gloriously large apartment and we gave a handful of parties for friends who'd also stayed on in New Haven for the summer. That was how I learned a simple trick to turn pasta into an elegant party meal: the secrets of Pasta Primavera.

One boils penne as usual, and at the same time cleans, peels (when necessary) and dices carrots, peppers, peas, and similar types of sweet vegetables. It's best to avoid celery, which is overpowering, but broccoli, zucchini, and squash can all be added according to taste. When the pasta is ready, drain, and then put it back in the pot. Over a low flame, toss the pasta with olive oil, garlic, and the diced vegetables. Then place the mixture into a lidded casserole dish, and cover with a thick layer of mozzarella. Bake for 5 to 10 minutes, and serve immediately. With a fresh loaf of bread and a salad, this makes a simple, elegant-looking meal. It's even easy enough that I've made it for myself on nights when I wasn't expecting guests.

Whether you are dining alone or with company, may you find among the following recipes a crowning jewel for your table.

Note: Noodle Kugel is made with pasta, as its name implies, but is a dish I've always considered to be a dessert. I've known it to be served at any number of points during a meal, so I, by editorial fiat, put Robert Glück's Noodle Kugel in the catch-all category at the end of the book. Also, look for Carol Queen's Smoked Salmon and Hazelnut Fettucine swimming with the other fish recipes.

L.S.

Michael Musto

In my stereotypically Italian family, cooking is a woman's pride, her all-the-stops-out means of expressing love. Devour a hefty portion of my mother's lasagna and it shows you love her back. Refuse it and you're driving a giant knife through her heart. I drove a knife through Mama's heart when I showed up at a pot-luck party last year with my own tray of Trés Gay Lasagna. As everyone ravenously sucked my offering down and raved about it to no end, she didn't seem to be beaming with maternal pride at all—in fact, the woman was resentful and jealous! I had taken over her job, co-opted her skill, clutched at her artery-clogging kudos. But, in all innocence, I couldn't help having adapted the lasagna trick to my own needs, and after all I'd learned from the master. And, except for a boiled egg or a Cup o' Noodles, it's the only damned thing I can make. To me, my lasagna is a way of presenting something so intricate and delicious it couldn't help but garner sincere appreciation, but to my mother it was a subversive act that brazenly defied the gender roles of my family. I like that idea too—but I think once she takes a bite, my mother will stop being so angry about the whole thing.

Trés Gay Lasagna

2 one-pound boxes lasagna
noodles
A tad of olive oil
1 onion
8 to 10 small cans tomato
sauce
4 small cans tomato paste
Salt, pepper, Italian spices
1 clove garlic
2 twelve-ounce containers
ricotta cheese
2 eggs
2 twelve-ounce mozzarella
cheeses
A dab of butter
Parmesan cheese

Boil the lasagna noodles in a large pot of water, with a tad of olive oil to keep them from sticking. When they seem ready, drain the water and dry the noodles.

Meanwhile, slice an onion into thin slices and, after lightly sautéing them, mix them into another large pot with the tomato sauce, tomato paste, salt, pepper, and spices (including bits of garlic). After bringing the sauce to a boil, keep it simmering on a very low flame for 20 minutes or so, stirring intermittently.

In a big bowl, mix the ricotta cheese with two eggs, plus salt and pepper. And in another bowl, slice up the mozzarella into small cubes. Coat the bottom of a big aluminum tray with a thin smidge of butter. Then put enough of the sauce on it to comprise one layer. Then lay down a layer of noodles, in whichever direction you like. Then spread a layer of the ricotta mix, then a layer of the mozzarella cubes, then more sauce, and so on until the pan is full. Bake at approximately 350 degrees for 40 minutes or until it feels firm in the middle.

Have extra sauce and some Parmesan cheese ready to throw on top.

Cultural critic and drag queen, **MICHAEL MUSTO** is a longtime gossip columnist for *The Village Voice*, and also hosts an E! Entertainment Television show, when he's not busy being a pop icon.

Lucy Jane Bledsoe

For Christmas this year, my partner's mother gave me a very colorful tablecloth with a pattern of big apples, green leaves, and white blossoms. "So you can have your editors to lunch," she told me. I love picturing "my editors" sitting at my poor kitchen table covered with that postmodern riot of apples— what would I serve them? The tablecloth definitely calls for bottles of hearty red wine, hunks of smelly cheese, crusty bread. And maybe a big plate of pasta.

This clam-sauce linguini has tricked several friends into thinking I've made them a gourmet meal. In fact, it takes ten minutes to prepare.

LUCY JANE BLEDSOE is the author of *Sweat: Stories and a Novella* and editor of *Heatwave: Lesbians in Love and Lust,* among other books.

Mock Gourmet Clam Sauce Linguini

2 cloves garlic, minced
6 to 10 scallions, chopped
2 tablespoons olive oil
1 ten-ounce can whole baby
    clams, or a couple dozen
    fresh clams
1 tablespoon cornstarch
$\frac{1}{8}$ to $\frac{1}{4}$ cup dry white wine
1 tablespoon lemon juice
Salt and freshly ground pepper
$\frac{1}{2}$ packed cup chopped
    parsley
Freshly grated Parmesan
    cheese

Sauté the minced garlic and chopped scallions in the olive oil until soft, about 5 minutes. Meanwhile, drain the juice from the can of clams into a small bowl. Thoroughly stir the cornstarch into the clam juice.

Once the garlic and scallions are cooked, add the clams and sauté for about 30 seconds. Add the clam juice and stir sauce thoroughly. Slowly add the wine and lemon juice, tasting as you go for the desired amounts. Let simmer until sauce thickens slightly, about 5 or 10 minutes.

Salt lightly and grind plenty of fresh pepper into the sauce. Serve over linguini. Sprinkle with chopped parsley and freshly grated Parmesan cheese. Serves two to four.

Note: If you use fresh clams, stir the cornstarch into lemon juice before adding it to the sauce. Throw the clams, shells and all, into the sauce and sauté until the clams open fully. Discard any clams that do not open.

Laura Antoniou

Spaghetti sauces are personal things—I like mine with lots of chunks of meat and mushrooms, and a heavy hand on the garlic. I cook this for women who I want to impress—and then hope that they'll be so impressed they'll never ask me to cook anything else. Serve this with warm, crusty Italian bread, garlic bread if you like, and a robust salad with onions and good balsamic vinegar.

Laura's Never Fail, Amazingly Rich & Chunky Tomato Sauce

1 to 2 tablespoons olive oil (Use the good stuff!)
1 large onion, chopped
3/4 pound white or wild mushrooms, thinly sliced
3 cloves garlic, minced or chopped
1/2 cup flavorful red wine
2 twenty-eight-ounce cans crushed Italian plum tomatoes
1 three-ounce can tomato paste
1/4 cup water

3 tablespoons chopped fresh basil, or 2 tablespoons dried
1 tablespoon chopped fresh or dried parsley
1 teaspoon oregano
1 teaspoon salt or salt substitute
Freshly ground black pepper to taste
1 pound chopped meat (optional)
    I use good ground beef, because I don't eat pork or veal. But you can use veal or sweet Italian sausage, if you like.

Place a large saucepan over medium heat for about a minute. Add the olive oil, onion, and mushrooms, and sauté, stirring often, until they start to get soft.

Add the garlic and a sprinkling of the basil. Stir, and cook for another minute or two.

Increase the heat and add the wine (watch for splatters!), and then cook until the liquid is reduced by half. Then, stir in the tomatoes, the paste, water, and the rest of the basil, the parsley, oregano, salt, and pepper.

When the sauce begins to bubble, turn the heat down to low, cover the pot, leaving a steam vent open, or propping the lid with a wooden spoon, and let the sauce simmer. Stir occasionally, but keep it cooking for at least 45 minutes, preferably an hour. Cooking it longer will thicken the sauce and make it more flavorful.

Tips and variations: If you are making a meat sauce, brown your meat in a frying pan over high heat with a sprinkling of basil, salt, and pepper. Drain the fat off, and add the meat to the sauce when you add the crushed tomatoes.

If you don't eat meat, you can add a can of flaked tuna for a different taste and texture. Or, add more garlic, 2 tablespoons of capers, a dozen or so pitted, black olives, a six-ounce can roasted Italian peppers, and more pepper, and make it a puttanesca-style sauce.

If you like a sauce with even more body, add ½ cup grated Romano or Parmesan cheese during the simmering stage.

This sauce improves after sitting in the fridge over night. It also freezes very well. Use small containers, so it defrosts quickly, and you'll have a handy last-minute supper anytime you need one.

LAURA ANTONIOU is the author or editor of numerous books, including *Looking for Mr. Preston, Leatherwomen I* and *II, Some Women,* and, under the byline Sara Adamson, the Marketplace Trilogy.

Pam Keesey

Anti-Vampire Garlic Pasta with Fresh Herbs

1 pound pasta
6 quarts water
3 tablespoons olive oil
8 to 16 cloves garlic, coarsely minced
2 cups fresh basil and parsley, finely
   chopped
1 to 2 cups cream
Lemon juice
Freshly ground pepper
Freshly grated Italian or Argentine
   Parmesan

Your friends have all tired themselves out and are heading home. It's last call and you're still alone, not at all what you had planned. As bodies sway to the final soft strands of music, you see her. She steps out from the dark depths of the club. She couldn't have been here all night, and certainly not alone. No—you certainly would have noticed her before now. Dark hair, black as coal; eyes the deepest of midnight hues; porcelain skin and lips as red as.... Her black-clad form is moving, lithely, gracefully, and, yes, even seductively, across the dance floor. How could you not notice her?

"Are you alone?" she asks. She's talking to you! Your knees go weak. Your heart is pounding; you feel flushed, overheated, electric. "Shall we get a bite to eat? How about your place?" she says liltingly, enchantingly. You stammer. A question forms in your mind, but can't seem to find its way out of your mouth. She takes your hand and leads you out into the night.

56

"Aren't you going to invite me in?" she says. You stop. Your voice, which had abandoned you the minute you looked into her eyes, is struggling to be let free.

"Please. Come in," you say, gesturing grandly, waving your hand across the threshold.

While you search the refrigerator, she pours you a glass of wine. Red wine. She places the glass in your hand. "To the Children of the Night," she says as you touch your glass to hers. You take a sip, turning back to the task at hand. From the depths of the refrigerator an idea comes to you. But then the question forms in your mind: Do you really want to know?

You plunge 1 pound of pasta into 6 quarts of boiling water. Enough for 4, you realize, but you have no idea how hungry you really are. Or how hungry she might be. In a small frying pan, you heat 3 tablespoons of olive oil, adding 8, no 10, how about 12? Damn it all, you add all 16 cloves of garlic that have been coarsely minced. If this doesn't work, you think, nothing will.

On a low heat, you gently sauté the garlic, watching it closely as it turns a light, even translucent brown. Your mind wanders to that lovely creature sipping her wine in the living room as you toss the pasta with the sautéed garlic and 2 cups of finely chopped basil and parsley. What if it is true, you wonder as you gently stir in 1 to 2 cups of cream, mixing the pasta and adding the cream until a little sauce forms around the pasta itself. Do you really care if it is true?

You taste the pasta, adding just a bit of lemon juice, some freshly ground pepper, and topping it all with freshly grated Italian or Argentine Parmigiana cheese. "A little midnight snack," you announce as you serve generous portions to both yourself and the gorgeous denizen across the table.

Now is the moment of truth. But wait! She doesn't cringe! She's not backing away! She twirls her fork amidst the pasta, bringing the creamy forkful to her ruby lips. She opens her moist mouth and takes it all in, chewing ever so lightly, ever so subtly. "Delicious," she says.

You sigh, relaxed, relieved. "Such a meal deserves a kiss," she says. You feel her arms around you, the light brush of her breath on your mouth, her warm lips on your cheek, her creamy, garlic-scented mouth on your neck. She sinks her teeth in.

PAM KEESEY is the editor of *Daughters of Darkness, Dark Angels,* and *Women Who Run with the Werewolves,* and author of the forthcoming *Vamps: An Illustrated Guide to Women as Vampires.* She lives in Minneapolis.

Tony Kushner

I don't think any single paragraph I've written has gotten as much positive response as the lasagna description from my OutWrite Keynote Address. I suppose this means we're all very hungry. So people now assume that I have the secret to the lasagna pie of their dreams. Beautiful men are constantly forcing their attentions upon me, offering me sexual favors in return for a home-cooked meal; scarcely a night goes by when I don't have to shoo some gym bunny out of my bed who's crawled there in the vain hope of getting me to whip him up some of my mama's runny, yummy, vein-clogging casserole.

But even the most toothsome of these beauties go away unfulfilled. I can't make them lasagna, I no longer make lasagna, not for anyone. Because I have, since I made that speech, transformed my diet and myself, having eliminated all fat from my diet and in the process having lost one hundred pounds. It's basically the Dean Ornish regimen as outlined in his book Eat More, Weigh Less. *The system gives a chronic overeater like myself an edible substance (fat) upon which it is possible to pronounce the same anathema with which an alcoholic permanently abolishes alcohol—no more, never again, not even a drop. I will never eat fat again. No meat, almost no fish (shrimp and scallops are okay), no oils of any sort, no butter and no real cheeses. I decided that, since I work in theater, I should be able to do this: when I see a great production I have to live with the fact that I will never see it again, once it's closed and gone forever. People who love theater love having memories, and can live off them; so I figure I should be able to live off the memory of what a feta cheeseburger tastes like, just like I must live off the memory of watching the divine Charles Ludlam onstage, because Charles is gone and for my health and well-being, so too must feta cheeseburgers.*

The superiority of the Ornish no-fat-forever regimen resides in the fact that it isn't a diet. You never go off it. You don't have to mediate, there are no choices to make; instead of hearing my mother saying, "Have another slice of lasagna!" and diving in, I simply hear her saying, recalling her voice from an earlier part of my life, "NO NO NO!" And suddenly I, who have never been able to control my eating, am eating healthy and copiously, and for two years now I've been losing weight and maintaining, and so lasagna is a thing of the past.

My cousin, Dot Edelstien, has made a rather tasty vegetarian non-fat lasagna for me—and this is the catch—non-fat cheeses. These are curious foodstuffs; they taste to me like cheese that dreams of being toothpaste when it grows up. They're not made with that horrible synthetic fat mega-molecule the corporations have dreamed up, the one that apparently looks like fat on a potato chip and acts, sorry to be vulgar, like a high colonic. These cheeses don't taste chemical, and I've noticed no alarming gastro-intestinal sequelae, but they do taste slightly defeated, unhappy: the party's over, they've taken the moon (and the cheese it's made of) away.

Mary Louisa

Spinach
Non-fat vegetable stock, or red
    wine
Onions
Garlic
Several varieties of
    mushrooms, including
    some nice big meaty
    portobellas
Spices (see the speech) to
    taste
Tomatoes
Tomato paste or sauce
    (optional)
Lasagna noodles
Non-fat cheeses, such as
    Swiss, ricotta, mozzarella,
    cottage cheese and
    Parmesan

Sauté the spinach in non-fat vegetable stock, or in red wine; it takes very little heat to wilt it and make it tender. Then set it aside; do a separate pan of the onions and garlic made tender in wine or stock; then add in the mushrooms, sliced into bite-sized pieces, and the spices, and the tomatoes, having boiled them briefly, skinned them, and pulverized them. You may want to add in tomato paste or sauce as long it has no added oil. Stir in the spinach and let this all simmer till everything's tender.

Having boiled your noodles (read the box) (or get fresh noodles and boil them till al dente) get a very deep casserole dish, smear a little tomato sauce on the bottom, and begin layering. I go one layer of noodles, one layer of the ragout, cheese, noodles, etc., for three layers minimum. The secret is in neither skimping nor putting too much in—again see the essay: you will find your lasagna is as excessive or as balanced or as tight-assed as you yourself tend to be. Sometimes its character is shaped by its intended, by the person for whom it is being cooked. I do not have a method of construction I can share with you, it's really a lot like playwriting, you have to learn by doing it and arrive at a look for the pie that pleases you: do not worry what John Simon will say. Each slice theoretically should stand tall until forked, and then slowly yield up its treasures as the meal moves towards its gastronomic Elysium. As much Elysium, at any rate, as a meal cooked without fat can attain. I won't pretend this is without sacrifice. Life has lost some of its lubrication. The gold patina's been stripped off the walls a bit, revealing something underneath the color of bone; but as I move towards forty I accept it, embrace it, even. I have my memories. And the fat cells never die.

The Zucchini Addendum: One might also add thin or thick slices of zucchini and yellow squash, sautéed in wine with some fennel and oregano, which when tender is added to the spinach ragout. There are also the tofu/seitan/tempeh meaty-tasting soy products; I haven't found that these manage to maintain their meat-masquerade under oven heat. But I don't really know how to work with them; they make me too forlorn for the real carnal thing.

TONY KUSHNER is the award-winning playwright of numerous works, including the epic *Angels in America: A Gay Fantasia on National Themes*, for which he won the Pulitzer Prize in 1993; *A Bright Room Called Day*; *Slavs!*; and numerous others. His OutWrite speech, "On Pretentiousness," which contains the paragraphs on lasagna as his paradigm for writing a play, can be found in his book *Thinking about the Longstanding Problems of Virtue and Happiness*. It even lists all the ingredients for his original opulent, garlicky, garrulous, promiscuous, flirtatious, insistent, persistent, overwhelming, exhaustive, and exhausting lasagna.

Everything but the Girl:

Fish

PERSONALLY, I AM HIGHLY ALLERGIC to eating any kind of fish (I go into shock). As I was growing up, I wanted nothing more than to be a marine biologist, but it became patently unfeasible the first time I went out on a research boat during high school and got severely sick. I've even had allergy attacks from kissing men who'd recently dined on fish, especially tuna—and they thought they were such good kissers they'd knocked my socks off, as it were.

Seafood lovers, however, will undoubtedly want to dive into the waters of these scrumptous dishes.

L.S.

Achy Obejas

LISA (LEFT) AND ACHY OBEJAS

*P*rior to Lisa, my lover, stepping foot into my apartment, I had no dining-room table (I ate at my desk, watching TV, in bed...), a lumpy old torn-up couch, and nothing on the walls.

I'd been living in the place for a year, a kind of reclusive, Spartan existence after a couple of years with a male roommate in another apartment. Now, alone, I had a view of the lake; I could write at all hours. I was happy.

Then I start seeing Lisa. Her place is comfy, lover-friendly, the TV's in the right place, she has matching drinking glasses and a pair of cuddly cats. I realize immediately I need to buy some time before I can let her come over.

So I create a myth about how no one ever comes over to my place, that I'm really particular about my space, that I'm an anti-social creep. I manage to pull this off for close to a month—it helped mightily that I was at an artists' colony in Virginia for part of that time. In the meantime, I'm saving money.

Finally, I realize I cannot put this off any longer. She's asking questions, looking hurt, wondering if I live in a sniper's cross-fire—or if, perhaps, I'm a secret sniper, a psycho, a drooling lesbo pedophile.

I use my trusty Montgomery Ward credit card to buy a dining-room set and I pull some monies from savings and buy a couch. The couch arrives immediately.

63

An old girlfriend—an art dealer with exquisite taste who wants me to please settle down and have a normal life—comes over and we put up my art collection (believe it or not, I actually have a modest one—I mean, real art).

The next day, I'm panicking. The guys from the homeless shelter haven't come over to pick up the old couch and Montgomery Ward can't deliver the dining-room set until after Lisa's scheduled to come over (she's picking me up to take me to the airport).

I recruit my neighbor, a black Christian dyke opera singer who keeps trying to get me into her New Age church (I almost promised to go), and we rush to Montgomery Ward. The dining-room set is in pieces in different boxes. We have to tie it to the roof of my car with shoelaces and belts and drive ten miles an hour on the way home.

We rush in, recruiting gang guys from the neighborhood to bring in the boxes (we're both femme weaklings, a total disservice to the community)—that's right, I invite guys with colors right into my apartment so they can scout my computer and fax and make plans to steal them later. Mercifully, one of them recognizes me from some gang summit and tells me he thinks I'm cool and I, probably erroneously, feel relieved.

Then, of course, I have no tools, so we have to go knocking from door to door to get the right screwdriver to put this sucker together. As I'm busy screwing things in place, the shelter guys show up and haul the old couch away. My black Christian dyke opera singer neighbor throws all the boxes from the dining-room set off the fire escape (couldn't have them in my apartment or the hallway...of course, it didn't dawn on me she'd just blow them into the alley eleven floors down...).

Finally, it's ready. Lisa's due in ten minutes. I wash my face, change clothes, toss a few things around to make the place look lived in. By the time she walks through the door, I am breathless but casually playing Tetris at my computer.

"Wow," she says, "what a great place you have."

A couple of weeks later, I have her over for dinner with some friends. I serve this paella.

We now live together in a huge three-bedroom apartment with two wood-burning fireplaces and a jacuzzi.

Draw your own conclusions.

Seafood Paella

1 ¼ cup olive oil
2 onions, chopped
2 large green peppers, chopped
4 cloves garlic
Seafood: 3 whole crabs, cut in pieces; 2 lobster tails, cut in pieces; 1 pound shrimp; ½ pound crayfish; 1 to 2 cans smoked oysters (This is my preferred mix, but almost any variety will work.)
2 bay leaves
1 eight-ounce can tomato sauce
2 tablespoons black pepper
1 tablespoon vinegar
2 cups white wine
A dash of salt
4 cups vegetable or chicken broth
2 pounds rice
½ pound peas

In a huge pot, make a sofrito with the olive oil, onions, green pepper and garlic. Stir over a medium flame until the onions are soft and nearly transparent.

Add the seafood and bay leaves, and stir until everything is well mixed and the seafood has absorbed the sofrito. Add the tomato sauce, black pepper, vinegar, and white wine. Stir. Add a dash of salt. Stir.

When this mix boils, add the broth and rice. Cook 30 to 40 minutes, as you would rice.

In a separate pot, boil the peas until tender. When the paella's ready to be served, add the peas and stir. Serve directly from the pot.

Buen provecho!

ACHY OBEJAS is the author of the collection of stories *We Came All the Way from Cuba So You Could Dress Like This?* and the novel *Memory Mambo*. She lives in Chicago.

Lawrence D. Mass

𝒥im Owles was the founding president of Gay Activists Alliance (New York) and of the Gay and Lesbian Independent Democrats (GLID). He was the first openly gay person to run for public office in New York City and was a co-founder of the Gay and Lesbian Alliance Against Defamation (GLAAD). He was the gay liaison to Senator Manfred Ohrenstein. Owles is perhaps best known as the co-author and first presenter of the New York City gay civil-rights bill. Beloved friend and leader of our community, he died from complications of AIDS on August 6, 1993.

Jim used to love my lobster salad, which I made especially for him.

LAWRENCE D. MASS, M.D., is co-founder of Gay Men's Health Crisis (GMHC) and author of *Dialogues of the Sexual Revolution* and *Confessions of a Jewish Wagnerite*. He lives in Manhattan with his partner, Arnie Kantrowitz.

Lobster Salad for Jim Owles

2 ears corn on the cob
4 small new potatoes
I Bermuda onion
I close-to-ripe, medium-sized peach (or pear) that is still firm
I pound cooked lobster chunks
I lemon
$\frac{1}{2}$ teaspoon honey Dijon mustard
Balsamic vinegar
2 tablespoons salad oil
Mayonnaise (or sour cream)
Finely chopped parsley, basil, and mint
4 hot dog rolls
Margarine
Fresh tomatoes and avocados (optional)

Scrape the hard, uncooked corn from the cob, then cook it (about 2 minutes in boiling water or steam; do not overcook). Let it stand or cool in the refrigerator to room temperature. Wash and cut the new potatoes into small chunks, then cook them (about 5 minutes in boiling water or steam) and let them stand or cool in the refrigerator to room temperature.

Cut the Bermuda onion and the firm peach (or pear) into small pieces. Combine the cooked lobster chunks with several generous squeezes of lemon, a $\frac{1}{2}$ teaspoon honey Dijon mustard, several generous splashes of balsamic vinegar, and 2 tablespoons of salad oil. Mix the combination gently and allow it to marinate for $\frac{1}{2}$ hour.

Then combine all of the ingredients and gently mix in the mayonnaise and/or sour cream. The mixture should be creamy but chunky. Add dashes of parsley, basil, and mint, and salt to taste.

Butter the hot dog buns (with butter or margarine) and toast them lightly. Serve the salad on the buns. Alternatively, serve the salad on avocado halves with fresh tomatoes. (Slices of avocado and tomato can also be placed with the salad on the buns.)

Ellen Kushner

Everything but the Grill

The early years of my adult life were spent on the Upper West Side of Manhattan, back when it was still considered a borderline place to live—and, in fact, my life there was the inspiration for Riverside in Swordspoint—something people who know the area now find hard to believe! Fresh herbs back then were a luxury. Now that I'm in Boston, my yard is full of thyme and sage and all manner of good things; in fact, I'm weeding out the mint that I used to sigh over at the Korean groceries!

Picture me, then, if you will, the Complete Outdoorswoman, taking every available summer evening to grill something over charcoal. Usually it's fish. To make it taste more interesting, I like to soak it in something flavorful first. I get extra points for using what I've got growing in the yard.

And so was born Green Marinade.

ELLEN KUSHNER is a nationally syndicated radio host, as well as author of the gay fantasy novel *Swordspoint,* among other books. She lives in Boston.

Green Marinade
(Everything in it is green...)

Fresh lime juice
Olive oil
Fresh basil leaves
Fresh (spear)mint leaves
Fresh chives, if you like
1 clove garlic, freshly pressed
   or smashed (Well, it was
   green once.)

Mix it all up in the dish you're going to put your fish in. It doesn't have to be a lot; the juice of one lime will do, plus a dash of olive oil. (A little less olive oil if you've got a fattier fish, like swordfish or tuna.) We're talking just a few leaves of each plant, here, for a pound of fish. Chop them or just crush them to get them to release their flavor.

Lay the filets in the marinade. Coat both sides; they don't have to be drowning in it, as long as they're well-exposed to the marinade. Cover the dish with plastic wrap so it doesn't stink up the fridge, and keep it cold until ready to grill or broil.

Thick steaks of fish only get more flavorful the longer you leave them in the marinade; 24 hours maxes out, and the lime juice may even begin to cook the fish all by itself. For a thinner (and more affordable) filet, like flounder or sole or even tilapia, an hour or so is enough to get the point across. Turn filets over once during the "soaking" time. Grill or broil them, and don't overcook!

Note: I've become a Smoking Fool. Just before you put the fish on the grill, lay some wood chips on the charcoal. If you've soaked them in water for at least 30 minutes already, they'll smolder and smoke, imparting their flavor to whatever you've got on there. You can buy little bags of pre-chipped hickory, mesquite, whatever; a friend's pear tree has also provided some wonderful scentsations! Same friend tells me you can put a dish of wood chips 'n' water on the bottom of your oven and get a good flavor into roasted things in the winter. We'll see about that.

Carol Queen

Smoked Salmon and Hazelnut Fettucine

Needless to say, the better the quality of the smoked salmon you use, the more fabulous this dish will be.

Prepare fettucine according to package directions. While it's boiling, heat the olive oil in a pan and sauté the shallots and garlic. When they're soft, combine the salmon, lemon zest, and any of the herbs, warming them through. Toss the oil-salmon mixture with the fettucine and hazelnuts. (If you didn't use lemon zest, squeeze the lemon over the mixture now and toss a little more.)

All you really need to go with this dish are good bread and a salad. Serves four to six.

1 package fettucine, preferably something opulent like basil- or spinach-flavored
1 cup smoked salmon, minced or shredded (more if you're a pig)
½ cup chopped or Cuisinarted hazelnuts
4 cloves chopped shallots, or to taste
Chopped garlic to taste
1/2 cup olive oil
Lemon or lemon zest
Dill, basil or oregano to taste (optional)

CAROL QUEEN is the author of *Exhibitionism for the Shy* and co-editor of *Switch Hitters: Lesbians Write Gay Male Erotica and Gay Men Write Lesbian Erotica* and the forthcoming *PoMoSEXUALS*. A sex-positive activist and safer-sex educator, she regularly gives lectures and workshops around the country (and the world), has appeared in numerous videos, and works at Good Vibrations.

Chicken and Other Jailbait:

Poultry and Eggs

I DON'T PROPOSE TO ANSWER WHICH CAME FIRST, the chicken or the egg; both find a home in this section. And both were very much a part of my home, as I was growing up. We had a large white longhorn rooster named Alpo who lived in our kitchen for eight years, a remarkable longevity for a fowl. Alpo earned his moniker because he loved to eat kibbles out of my sister's rottweiler's bowl, when the dog was fed out back. Alpo ranged outdoors whenever he desired, visiting his harem of hens, but spent most of the winter perched atop the wire dog cage in the kitchen (he pecked on the side door when he desired entrance), watching us dine or cook and occasionally commenting loudly on these actions (he crowed at whim, having no understanding of timing or sunrise) and always hoping for table-scraps of any sort. Chickens can be amazingly carnivorous, and many a time I've watched them devour a broken egg, especially yolk and shell, for the nutrients and the calcium.

When I lived in Granada one summer, learning to dance flamenco, I was fed an egg a day, at least, because people didn't know what else to feed a vegetarian. One of my favorite dishes was the tortilla español, a potato and onion frittata that can be eaten hot or cold, and is usually cut and served like a pie or cake. I tried to recreate it, and though I had watched it prepared often while I was in Spain, I was unable to make it in the U.S. until I learned a few secrets from my friend, Tim Sutton, who'd also lived in Spain but had taken better notes on how to make a tortilla.

The most important revelation that Tim shared was his frying pan, an eight-inch omelet pan, and that made all the difference. So much in this recipe is based on personal and subjective experience.

Both potatoes and eggs come in a wide range of sizes, so it's hard to give exact numbers: not too many potatoes, which are the bulk of this dish, and not too many eggs so that it's runny. A good way to decide how much you need is to peel and cube your potatoes until they fill your omelet pan. You'll then want two or three eggs, enough to cover all the potatoes.

To begin, sauté one medium onion and two or three cloves of garlic in olive oil, then remove them from the oil and set them aside in a large bowl. Using the same oil (and more if necessary) sauté the potatoes. Remove them as well, and add them to the onions and garlic.

In a separate bowl, whisk the eggs until they're blended, and then add them to the potatoes and onion mixture, stirring until everything is well coated. Remove most of the oil from the pan, until only a thin coat is left, enough to keep the tortilla from sticking to the pan. Make sure the oil is hot before you add the mixture from the bowl, but also make sure the flame is on medium and not high, so that the tortilla cooks all the way through. You want to pour enough of the mixture into the pan so that it fills the pan, a good thickness. Shake regularly, in a circular motion, to keep the tortilla from burning to the sides. When it looks like it's starting to dry up, and the eggs are beginning to cook, put an upside-down plate on top and flip the entire pan over.

This was the second revelation, in that it's the tricky part that I'm always most intimidated by. It's best to place your hand over the bottom of the plate and flip the whole pan/tortilla/plate up and sort of around with your shoulder, catching it all on the now-right-side-up plate. This needs to be done quickly, and helps keep all the hot oil from leaking out and burning you. It's one of the reasons you want to remove most of the oil, except a thin layer to coat the sides, before adding the egg mixture. You may need to add some more oil to the pan, and wait for it to heat up, before sliding the tortilla off the plate and into the pan again. You can flip the tortilla a few times, but most of the cooking happens between the first and second flip, and that's really all you need. It's a flashy move, though, once you've got it down, and can truly impress a date or guest. It may be wise to practice with a cold pan and plate, first, until you're comfortable and not winding up with flying and shattered crockery, among other possible injuries.

Truly, this is not as dangerous as it sounds. For most of the recipes in this section, just grab a coq (or duck, where appropriate) and follow the directions.

L.S.

Kitty Tsui

I love to eat. Anyone who knows me or who has read my work knows this.

I will not go into a discussion of white rice versus brown, or present long-winded anecdotes. This dinner is quick and easy. You can arrive home from work, cook, shower, and change for a big date, and still have time to enjoy the evening. If things get hot and heavy when your date arrives and you don't sit down to dinner immediately, this is also good eaten cold. Believe me. I know.

KITTY TSUI is a wordsmith who loves food, women, and sex (probably in that order). In her leisure time (which isn't often), she frequents noodle shops, grocery stores, coffeehouses, restaurants, farmer's markets, cookware specialty stores, and flea markets searching for delicacies. Read her collection *Breathless* for more food (and sex) ideas.

Prelude to Decadence: Dinner for a Date in Under Fifty Minutes

Coq Au Kitty Tsui, a.k.a. Broiled Lime Caper Chicken

2 chicken breasts (with bone and skin)
1 tablespoon extra-virgin olive oil
1 lime
2 tablespoons capers

Marinate the chicken breasts (with the bone and skin) in extra-virgin olive oil, the juice of the lime, and the capers. They can be marinated overnight or for 30 minutes.

Broil them skin-side down for 15 minutes, then turn them and continue broiling for another 15. Do not overcook! Before serving, remove the skin. If you are using deboned breasts, cook for 25 minutes total or until no pink appears in the juice when the thickest part of the meat is pierced with a sharp blade.

White Rice

Put rice on to cook in the rice-cooker. You do have one, right? Every civilized household should. You can choose to skip the rice and stick with potatoes but I like rice with every meal. Besides, a little of the juice from the chicken is delicious spooned over rice.

Boiled New Potatoes and Steamed Asparagus

Boil some new potatoes and steam your asparagus. Easy does it. The important thing is not to overdo anything. When the potatoes are ready, sprinkle with ½ teaspoon of fresh dill.

If you can't find asparagus, use green beans, broccoli, cauliflower, or anything fresh. If you must use salt, do so sparingly. I try to avoid it myself.

Green Salad with Blue Cheese Dressing

Greens: any mixture of red- or green-leaf lettuce, arugula, romaine, Boston or butter lettuce, radicchio, or spinach
Cherry tomatoes
Freshly grated Parmesan
Freshly ground black pepper
Brianna's Homestyle True Blue Cheese Dressing

Whatever you do, do not use iceberg lettuce. That will not do! Wash the greens, and cut up some ripe cherry tomatoes. Tomatoes taste best (those that have any taste) ripened on your kitchen windowsill and kept unrefrigerated. Sprinkle with freshly grated Parmesan cheese and freshly ground black pepper just before serving.

I like blue cheese dressing myself. Brianna's Homestyle True Blue Cheese Dressing is my absolute favorite.

Grapes, Blood Oranges, and Kiwi Fruit

End the dinner with chilled seedless white grapes, and sectioned kiwi fruit and blood oranges.

I sometimes follow with a good cigar (Avo XO is my favorite), and a latte. But it depends on my mood and my plans for the evening.

Set a nice table. Fresh flowers are always good. As are candles. Tapers, please, not the fat kind you use in the bathroom or the bedroom. In my opinion, cloth napkins are a must. Ironed ones make a good impression—on me at least.

Bon appétit. Enjoy your dinner and your date.

Michael Denneny

his is my ever-trustworthy plan for those harried evenings when I leave the office at five-thirty and know I have four to six people coming to dinner at eight. Though basic—even downright plain—it works and it's fast. It also seems particularly popular with people with AIDS, who seem to do best with simple, non-spicy foods. It was Paul Monette's favorite meal at my house, one that he asked for each time he visited as if it were a gourmet treat.

A Perfect Dinner Party in Two Hours

The following shopping list provides the whole meal:

2 to 3 cans Campbell's tomato soup	Butter
Fresh bread	Parsley
4- to 6-pound roasting chicken	Lemons
2 to 3 acorn squash	Honey
Vegetables for steaming, such as carrots or Brussels sprouts	Lawry's Seasoned Salt
	Raisins (optional)
	Chocolate dessert

MICHAEL DENNENY has been a pioneer and founding father of the gay literary scene, helping to found *Christopher Street* magazine and creating St. Martin's Press' Stonewall Inn series focusing on gay and lesbian titles. He is also the author of *Decent Passions* and *Lovers: The Story of Two Men*, as well as numerous essays.

Tomato Soup

Use Campbell's tomato soup—it's the best they make, though do add 2 tablespoons of butter and whisk briskly while heating. Serve with a few springs of parsley on top, with a very thin circular slice of lemon floating in the middle, and with the very best loaf of freshly baked bread your neighborhood offers. (Eli's sourdough baguettes, for the Upper West Side of Manhattan.)

Roast Chicken

Wash the chicken inside and out in warm water, removing any innards; pat it dry with paper towels; massage the skin with half lemons and sprinkle (very) liberally with Lawry's Seasoned Salt. Put it on a rack in a roasting pan, or, better still, one of those vertical chicken-holder do-hickeys that lets all the fat drip off, and roast at 325 to 350 degrees for 18 to 20 minutes per pound. Basically, you shove it into the oven for an hour and 15 minutes, then look at it.

Acorn Squash

Cut each squash in half, scoop out the innards, perforate the flesh with a fork, drop a tablespoon of butter and a large dollop of honey in each hollow, then put them on a rack below the chicken rack and cook for an hour. (Squash is easy; 15 minutes more won't do it any harm; if the squash is done early, remove and cover with tin foil.)

Steamed Vegetables

Use a triple boiler with several steaming compartments. Cut carrots into 1-inch lengths and steam till slightly soft—say 45 minutes. You can add raisins if you want. Brussels sprouts will take about a half hour and will cook better if you remove the older outer leaves, cut off the stem and score it (cut an X into the stem). Both can be served with butter or lemon juice, or both.

Dessert

Take the easy way out and buy sherbet or ice cream or frozen yogurt and cookies (with chocolate somehow involved).

James Johnstone

I'm an adventuresome eater. I love to eat and drink well, and I love to cook. I tend to cook food that is spicy, color-ful. My repertoire is heavily influenced by Asian cooking. I love Malaysian, Indian, Szechwan, Indonesian, Korean, as well as Japanese food. I stud-ied at a Japanese university for two and a half years. I traveled all over the country and enjoyed all sorts of local delicacies like shishamo *(sun-dried roe-filled sardines, lightly roasted over an open flame served with a squeeze of lemon, then eaten whole, guts and all, head first),* karashi mentaiko *(cod roe, pickled in red hot chili peppers),* iki-zukuri *(sashimi cut from living fish, served artistically filleted on the poor fishes still quivering body), and* basashi *(raw horse meat.... Don't tell my mom!)*

Besides my university studies of Japanese history, calligraphy, and Japanese fencing, I took up Sadou—*no, not some exotic form of samurai torture, but The Way of Tea. My time in Japan, and my time spent studying Japanese tea culture, heavily influ-ence how I prepare food and entertain friends. I have literally* hundreds of Japanese ceramic plates and serving bowls of every shape, size, and glazing. I have over one hundred guinomi *sake* cups, which I collected on my travels throughout Japan. When I entertain, I use these dishes and bowls, always the best for my friends. If I am serving sake (the best sake is served cold or room temperature!), I encourage my friends to change guinomi *often* throughout the meal. That's part of the fun of it. If something breaks? Well, I enjoyed it while I had it. I never give these incidences a second thought. In Japan, they say okyakusama wa kamisama da, *the guest is a god, and that's how I like to cook for and entertain my friends.*

Mami's Coke Soy Chicken

4 cups Coca-Cola Classic
2 cups Japanese soy sauce
1 package dashi
Grated ginger to taste
Grated garlic to taste
¼ teaspoon chili oil
4 pounds chicken drumettes

Put all of the ingredients in a large soup pot, and bring to a boil. Skim off any foam that may come to the surface. Turn the heat down to medium and simmer for 1 to 2 hours, or until the chicken is cooked and tender but not starting to fall off the bone.

This can be served warm or cold. Great as a snack at parties or as part of a meal with rice.

JAMES C. JOHNSTONE is co-editor of *Queer View Mirror: Lesbian and Gay Short Short Fiction* and its sequel, as well as a volume of erotic gay short short stories, *Quickies.* He lives in Vancouver, BC.

PHOTO: MIDGE ELIASSEN

Nancy Garden

Families are special to all of us, of course—ties of blood and history, of people shared: eccentric uncles, flamboyant aunts, crazy cousins. But we gay folk are blessed with another, wider family, often closer than our blood families—our queer sisters and brothers, with whom we share not blood, but coming out stories, a common vocabulary, the pain of invisibility, otherness, bashings and AIDS; the joy of Pride, and the love, for all our bickering, that makes us feel instantly at home with our own kind.

And like all families, we share celebrations and food.

For my partner, Sandy, and me, this has meant wonderful ethnic dinners with our good friends Joan and Claire (the less said about the famous Disappearing Dumplings the better!), Lobster Newburg and Southern fried chicken (not at the same time!) with our other good friends Dorrie and Diann—and most of all, Newmas (that's Christmas and New Year's combined)

NANCY GARDEN is the author of numerous children's books, including *Annie On My Mind*, a lesbian young adult novel that is one of the most-frequently banned books in this country. She lives in Massachusetts, with her partner, Sandy.

dinners with Barb and Win, who, over some thirty years, have shared all the joys and sorrows of our lives.

Newmas started in defiance, when we all had difficult and/or closeted relationships with our blood families and needed a holiday celebration in which we could be ourselves. Even back before we invented Newmas, when we were young and poor, we always got together sometime during the Christmas season to feast and to exchange the Ugly Presents—the worst, funniest, and most tasteless horrors we could find. I remember out-of-register Kennedy plates, a purple waterlily-shaped bath sponge, plastic fruit. As we got older, our celebrations got more serious and traditional—except for the different Newmas trees: a decorated ribbon outline on the door, a lovingly trimmed pineapple, and the various hemlock branches festooned with seed pods and pine cones.

Newmas dinner evolved with the holiday, and has changed some in these fat-, cholesterol-, and sugar-conscious days. But central in it for many years was:

The Newmas Duck

1 cup orange juice
1 large duckling
Garlic

Heat the orange juice. Wash the duckling, trim the excess fat from its cavity (save the giblets for gravy), and rub the duck with garlic inside and out. Stuff with the stuffing described in the next recipe, and roast 20 to 30 minutes per pound at 300 degrees, basting every 10 minutes with the orange juice.

Stuffing

1 small to medium onion, chopped
1 large stalk celery, chopped
1 McIntosh apple, peeled, cored, quartered and sliced
Butter or margarine
About ⅓ cup raisins
About ⅓ cup pignoli
Marjoram, rosemary, sage
1 package Pepperidge Farm cornmeal stuffing

While heating the water and butter or margarine for the stuffing (follow the directions on package), sauté the onion, celery, and apple in butter or margarine in a large frying pan. Add raisins, nuts, and herbs, and stir in properly prepared Pepperidge Farm stuffing. Cool to a comfortable temperature for handling, then stuff and truss the duck.

Our other traditional Newmas recipe, which has been adapted from The New York Times Cookbook.

Barb & Win's Sweet Potato Casserole

4 clementines and tangerines (Clementines are sweeter, and may be seedless.)
6 medium sweet potatoes, cooked and peeled
¼ cup melted butter or margarine
6 tablespoons firmly packed brown sugar
3 tablespoons bourbon or dark rum
½ teaspoon salt
2 tablespoons chopped pecans

Peel the tangerines or clementines, removing the white membrane. (This takes forever!) Separate the sections, and divide those from two of the fruits into halves, removing the seeds. Set aside.

Mash the sweet potatoes and whip them with 2 tablespoons of the butter, 4 tablespoons of the brown sugar, the bourbon or rum, and the salt.

Fold the seeded, sectioned, and divided fruit into the sweet potato mixture, and put into a greased 2-quart casserole dish.

Carefully remove the seeds from the remaining fruit sections. (Small, sharp scissors help with this.) With these sections, decorate the top of the casserole.

Mix the remaining butter and brown sugar with the pecans, sprinkle over the casserole, and bake 30 minutes at 375 degrees. Serves six.

Lars Eighner

Soft Breakfast Tacos

8 flour tortillas
½ white onion, coarsely
    chopped
1 clove garlic, sliced and
    crushed
1 tablespoon cooking oil
4 eggs
1 to 3 (to taste) Serrano
    peppers, sliced finely
¼ teaspoon salt
¼ cup finely shredded
    Monterey Jack
¼ cup finely shredded
    cheddar
¼ cup sour cream
Sliced black olives
Cilantro sprigs

Steam the tortillas if you are not microwaving them. Sauté the onions and garlic in oil until translucent.

Beat the eggs until thoroughly mixed. Add the sliced peppers, salt, and cheese to the eggs and mix. Add the egg mixture to the onions and garlic. When the eggs begin to set, stir constantly. Cook until the eggs are no longer runny, but avoid scorching them.

If you are microwaving the tortillas, separate them and brush each one very lightly with water. Microwave them on high for 1 minute or until they are hot and soft.

Spoon equal portions of egg mixture onto the tortillas and roll them up. Decorate them with sour cream using a pastry bag, or spoon the sour cream on in equal portions. Garnish with sliced olives and cilantro sprigs. Serve with salsa. Serves four.

Variation: Smother with chili; garnish with chopped onion and finely shredded cheese.

LARS EIGHNER is the author of *Travels with Lizbeth, Gay Cosmos, American Prelude, Whispered in the Dark, B.M.O.C.,* and many other books. He lives in Austin, Texas.

Victoria A. Brownworth

PHOTO: TEE A. CORINNE

Queering the Quiche

Can there be a more queer dish than quiche? Quite simply, quiche is the Liberace of foods: it's what puts the B in brunch; it is as queer as a drag queen on the Castro, a bike dyke in Berkeley. What self-respecting lesbian or gay man doesn't understand the importance of knowing her/his way around this most fundamental of queer foods?

How did quiche get so queer? Well, it is French, so it comes from the same people who gave us condoms, cross-dressing, Edith Piaf, and La Cage aux Folles. *But I believe quiche is queer because it's cheap and easy, but looks fabulous and elegant. Quiche is queer because it makes you feel like a queen, even if you're a pauper. The ideal recipe to romance a date or impress a frenzied brunch crowd, quiche gives good meal.*

And like queers, quiche is incomparably diverse. While doing a stint in the domestic Peace Corps (VISTA), I shared a tiny house in New Orleans with two other idealistic VISTA volunteers—another lesbian and a straight man with

86

incredibly queer sensibilities. Our food allowance would only buy a week's worth of groceries—but it had to last for a month. Inevitably at month's end my roommates would beg me to create gastronomic silk purses out of sow's ears and make real meals out of whatever remained of our food. Red beans and rice, thin but spicy soups, biscuits, and the ever-flexible quiche became my culinary mainstays.

I never thought much about the expansive nature of quiche before New Orleans. An older lover had taught me how to cook; appalled that my seventeen-year-old vegetarian repertoire was limited to pasta and salad, she endeavored to expand my gastronomic horizons. Quiche was the first step. A brunch queen from way back, her tutelage began with the most important meal of the day (in bed, naturally). In the era before cholesterol phobia, quiche was ever the queer dish of choice.

Joan may have taught me the rudiments of cooking, but poverty and necessity taught me to invent. In New Orleans, I began to experiment with the quiche model and found nearly every wilting vegetable could be made into a work of art. I also learned you could make quiche for twenty for what it would cost to buy breakfast for two at the Hummingbird Diner where the roaches were the same size as the fabulous biscuits and just as plentiful. Quiche was taffeta for the price of potato sacking.

Like queers themselves, quiche has many guises. Brunch may be its natural habillement, but quiche can dress for dinner as an appetizer or slip into something more comfortable for a late night supper. It can be simple and plain (not Jane, but Lorraine), or dramatic and quixotic, with a touch of the exotic. Quiche has perfect queer appeal—great presentation, with substance beyond surface. And quiche is good food—nutritious as well as delicious.

In New Orleans, my delectable yet ordinary quiches garnered accolades from my roommates, who lauded my culinary expertise. In New Orleans, I found quiche was very like being queer—it taught me how to adapt to circumstances.

Finally, quiche is no flash in the proverbial pan; quiche is chic but not trendy—it doesn't go out of fashion. Like torch songs and old movies, quiche is classic. And oh-so-queer.

VICTORIA A. BROWNWORTH is the author of seven books and editor of five, most recently *Too Queer, Night Bites,* and *Out for More Blood.* Her writing and commentary appear regularly in mainstream and queer publications, including *Out, Curve, The Village Voice, Ms.,* and *The Nation,* among others. She lives in Philadelphia with her partner, filmmaker Judith M. Redding.

All-Around Queer Quiche

Crust

1 ½ cups flour
Crisco Light
Freshly ground black pepper or
    cayenne (optional)
Crushed oregano or tarragon
    (optional)
A squeeze of lime juice
    (optional)

Use your own basic light pie crust or cut flour with Crisco Light (of course) until you have a ball of dough. Roll out thin (not too thin) and place in a greased quiche dish (if you don't have one, you should, but you can use a pie pan). Flute the edges.

If you want a more savory pie (this is especially good with meat, fish, or *quattro formaggio*) add a few pinches of freshly ground black pepper or cayenne, some crushed oregano or tarragon (never both), and a squeeze of fresh lime juice.

Custard

2 cups milk (not skim, but 2
    percent will work), half
    and half, or light cream
3 eggs (Calorie counters can
    use 1 whole egg and 2
    whites.)

Whisk ingredients together until creamy, frothy, and all the egg is mixed. Do this immediately before using; the egg will begin to separate if left standing. Add any herbs you are using directly to the custard.

Filling

Wonderfully flexible. As I suggest, you can make quiche with whatever is lying around (or even wilting) in the fridge. Other than soup, quiche is the best way to use leftovers. Use seasonal vegetables, bits of meat or fish (turkey, ham, salmon, roast beef), or even some exotic fruits (mango, star fruit, sliced black grapes) or flowers (nasturtiums, dandelion leaves, blooming basil, or dill) for a fabulous creation.

You need a full cup of vegetable or flesh. Adding some cheese ($\frac{1}{2}$ cup, diced or shredded) is optional, though the French would disagree. Match cheese to other components: Swiss with ham or mushrooms, ricotta with beef or fruit, mozzarella with spinach or sliced sweet onions, Monterey Jack with tomato slices or broccoli florets, Parmesan with asparagus spears or sliced peppers. Or if you feel your arteries are clear enough, use nothing but cheese: the best are Swiss, ricotta, sharp cheddar, and Parmesan in equal parts (*quattro formaggio*).

Line the crust with attractively arranged slices or bits of the vegetable/flesh of your choice. Cover this first layer with cheese, then carefully pour in custard to cover. With vegetables, float more on top of liquid. (This works well with mushrooms, fruit, tomato, zucchini, tiny broccoli florets.) With flesh, float some nice companionable herb (preferably fresh) on top—chives, parsley, basil—for aesthetics. With *quattro formaggio* dust the top with nutmeg or float some nasturtiums.

Other additions include garlic and onion, which are good with almost anything. Chives complement something light, like salmon. Tarragon is fabulous with tomato. So is basil. Rosemary will add an intriguing floral hint to turkey, zucchini, or green beans. Leave out salt—you can always add it later, if necessary.

Bake in a pre-heated 350-degree oven for 35 minutes or until the top begins to brown. Quiche is done when a knife inserted in the middle comes out clean. Allow it to set for 10 minutes before serving. Looks great. Reheats well. Serves six as a main dish, ten as an appetizer.

Note: Remember quiche is heavy. Serve with light salad, cold vegetable vinaigrette, a slice of smoked salmon, or fresh fruit. White wine, mimosas, or spicy virgin marys will complete the brunch, lunch, or late supper.

Beefcake:

Playing with Your Meats

THOUGH IT'S BEEN OVER A DECADE, and nearly half my life, since I've eaten meat, I still remember the taste of it very strongly. I gave up meat for health, rather than moral reasons; I'd been eating it three or four times a day, a typical red-blooded American-boy diet, which my body decided it did not approve of. So I became a vegetarian, and much later a fag and a femme, both of which are becoming viable options for a red-blooded American boy, the former more so than the latter.

If you do have a hankering for a piece of flesh, though, you've come to the right place.

L.S.

Richard Labonté

This hearty, low-maintenance, highly flexible dish was crafted during the nearly ten years I lived in a co-op household (that's upscale for a commune), where a dinner for just a few people might suddenly have to serve many—some with the munchies. It's basically an oven stew—and while it can expand to feed a lot of people, it'll also provide two people with tasty hot (turn it into a soup) or cold (top with chutney or grated cheese) leftovers for days. What I like about it is that it never tastes the same way twice, and because it bakes and steams instead of boiling and simmering, the flavor of the different meats and vegetables are much more (to use a cooking term...or it is a wine term?) robust.

RICHARD LABONTÉ returns annually (if not more frequently) to the co-op household in Canada where he developed this recipe. For nearly two decades, he has lived in the United States, where he is general manager for A Different Light bookstore, the largest gay and lesbian bookstore in the world, with stores in New York, San Francisco, and Los Angeles. A journalist for many years, he still reviews regularly for many periodicals, and is also the editor of *Best Gay Erotica 1997*.

The Loaves-and-Fishes Almost-Any-Meat (But No Fish) Meal

The Meat

4 to 6 chicken breasts
Or a 6- to 8-pound whole chicken
Or a 3- to 5-pound chunk of beef
(Because this is a slow-cook
dish, a cheap cut is fine.)
Or a 3- to 5-pound pork roast
Or a 5- to 6-pound lamb roast
Boneless is best but not essential.
Forget turkey: it doesn't meld
well with the other ingredients.

The Vegetables

Potatoes (any type, but small are
nice)
Onions (any type, or several)
Tomatoes (whole fresh are best,
but tinned are okay)
Carrots (from baby to big,
whatever)
Root veggies: parsnips, turnips,
rutabagas, baby squash
Bell peppers, cored and quartered
(any or all colors, depending
on the season)
Zucchini, whole
Fresh (best) or frozen Brussels
sprouts, broccoli, asparagus,
green beans, mushrooms
Garlic, more garlic, and then some
more (Fresh whole buds
preferred but juicy and crushed
from a jar will do; sprinkled
powder is a last resort.)
Peas, corn, beans (kidney, fava,
garbanzo), lentils, rice
Be creative: plantain, cored apples,
jícama
Avoid celery, radishes or cucumbers: they cloud the taste.

The Juices

Orange juice (for chicken or pork)
Tomato or vegetable juice (for beef)
Apple juice (for lamb or pork)

The Seasonings

Pepper (Let people add their own salt
at the table.)
"Salad" herbs: basil, rosemary,
tarragon, dill, etc.
A bit of fresh cilantro
Spices: Chinese five-spice or Thai
blend or Mexican blend; whatever
you have on hand
That stray package of powdered
potato-leek/ mushroom-barley/
minestrone/ whatever soup on the
shelf? Toss it in, too.

The Concept

By now I hope you get the point that,
though this dish is better when as
many fresh ingredients as possible are
used, it's also a clean-the-fridge deal as
well; and while the volume of meat is
finite, you can easily expand the serv-
ings by tossing in a couple more potatoes, a cup of rice, that aging tin of
kidney beans....

The Method

Heat your oven to 450 to 500 degrees.

Put the meat into the largest covered, oven-proof pot you have: remember, this is a dish with as many ingredients as you want. If your largest pot doesn't have a lid, several layers of tin foil will do (but check more often for possible charring).

Add a couple of cups of the appropriate liquid (and "reserve" a couple of cups for adding later if needed).

Sprinkle your choice of seasonings (except for cilantro, which should go in in the last few minutes).

Toss in the "hard" veggies: roots and tubers, potatoes, large whole onions.

Put the pot in the oven uncovered for 15 to 20 minutes, then cover and cook at 375 degrees for another 30 minutes.

Check the liquid level, add enough juice (or water) to keep an inch or two of liquid sloshing in the bottom. Add the "softer" fresh veggies: tomatoes, carrots, peppers, mushrooms, Brussels sprouts, asparagus, etc. Plus any rice or lentils. Any frozen or canned vegetables should be added about 30 minutes before you plan to serve the meal.

Cover the pot again and turn the heat down to 200 degrees.

Go read a book or have sex or visit with the people you are soon to feed, for about an hour. Or so. Check the pot a couple of times to make sure it's not cooking dry, and stir things around so the flavors blend.

The total cooking time is 100 to 120 minutes, half at low heat; if it cooks a bit longer, no problem.

When you are ready to eat, take the pot out of the oven, set it in the middle of the table, and serve—and do try to see that everyone at the table gets some of every vegetable if possible. It's nicer that way. For accompaniment: a good chewy bread with butter.

M.E. Kerr

John Fell, hero of the novels Fell, Fell Back, *and* Fell Down, *is a seventeen-year-old aspirant chef. Every Fell book includes one of his recipes. This one will be featured in the next.*

Fell's Meat Loaf

2 tablespoons butter
¾ cup chopped onion
1 pound ground beef,
    or ½ pound ground beef
    and ½ pound ground pork
1 teaspoon salt
1 teaspoon ground pepper
½ cup freshly chopped parsley
1 teaspoon Dijon mustard
1 egg, beaten
¾ cup dried bread crumbs
½ teaspoon thyme
4 slices bacon

Preheat oven to 350 degrees. Melt butter in a pan with onion and simmer until the onion is soft.

In a bowl, mix meat, salt, pepper, parsley, mustard, egg, bread crumbs, and thyme. Add butter and onions. Mix everything and make a loaf. Cover with bacon slices spread across the top.

Cook 1 to 1¼ hours, continuously pouring out any fatty juices in the pan. Loaf should not be sliced for 1½ hours after cooking. Serves four.

M.E. KERR is the award-winning author of many young adult novels, including *Deliver Us from Evie,* the first young adult novel that features a butch lesbian protagonist. She lives in East Hampton.

Tom Bianchi

TOM BIANCHI WITH HIS LOVER MARK PRUNTY

*W*hen I was first asked to submit a recipe for this project, I immediately thought of an easy tried-and-true rosemary roast chicken. This was a meal I often made for company. Most importantly, it was the first meal I used to seduce my life partner, Mark Prunty. As good as it is, it's too easy: salt and pepper, either a whole roaster or fryer, sprinkle with either fresh or dried rosemary needles, place on a rack roast for 20 minutes per pound at 350 degrees.

Mark turned out to be the more conscientious and inventive cook in our partnership. Therefore, I'm providing our favorite comfort food recipe—a wonderful meat loaf—which Mark makes for dinner parties when we really want our guests to know they're loved. In a world (especially in L.A.) where food style can get precious, a great meat loaf can be the equivalent of a well-designed basic black dress. This dish we lifted from a dinner party at our friend Michael Kleiser's.

Dinner Party Meat Loaf

2 ½ pounds ground beef
1 ½ pounds ground pork
2 slices bread, made into crumbs
½ cup oatmeal
4 eggs, beaten
2 teaspoons salt

1 tablespoon yellow mustard
1 cup tomato sauce
1 medium onion, chopped
1 five-ounce can of evap. milk
Fresh pepper

Mix all of the above ingredients in a bowl and form into a loaf in a large baking dish. Bake at 400 degrees for 1 hour, basting occasionally. Serves six with leftovers, unless the boys are real big.

Sauce

1 tablespoon dark brown sugar
1 cup tomato sauce
½ cup milk
4 tablespoons mustard
4 tablespoons vinegar

Warm all ingredients together in a sauce pan and serve on the side.

Photographer **TOM BIANCHI** is perhaps best known for his books on the bodybuilder couple Bob and Rod Jackson-Paris. His recent books include *In Defense of Beauty* and *Among Women*. He lives in Los Angeles with his life partner, Mark Prunty.

PHOTO: PHYLLIS CHRISTOPHER

Pat Califia

𝒲arning: This recipe can only be used if you have friends who are (1) not vegetarian, and (2) not the kind of clean-and-sober people who get freaked out about cooking with wine. (Other clean-and-sober people can safely partake, as any alcohol burns off during cooking.)

I know that I am advocating the death of a sentient being in order to put food on your table. Being a member of the Wolf Clan, I feel that eating meat is one of my sacred obligations. When I am dead, other creatures will eat my body. I feed the earth, which feeds me, and honoring that cycle is an important part of my spirituality. The goddess gives us life, but She also takes it away. As much as I deplore the excesses and cruelty of the meat industry, I also believe I cannot ignore my human heritage as a hunting pack animal. Ethically, we'd all be better off if we had to trek out into the wilderness and take down our own dinners, or hand-raise the animals that we personally had to kill and butcher for food. But the things I do to make the money that buys the pot roast are at least twice as hard. I respect the moral position that some people have taken as vegetarians. I just wish that more of them would not assume that people who eat meat have not wrestled with that dilemma, as well.

Probably the best-known lesbian erotic writer in America, **PAT CALIFIA** refuses to be pigeonholed, writing across any and all boundaries. She is the author of many classics, including *Macho Sluts, Doc and Fluff, Public Sex, Sensuous Magic,* and *Sapphistry,* among many others, and editor of *Doing It for Daddy, The Second Coming, The Lesbian S/M Safety Manual,* and other volumes.

Politically Incorrect Pot Roast

1 boneless cross-rib roast
Salt and pepper
1 bottle Gallo Hearty
     Burgundy
1 to 2 cans beef broth
1 yellow onion, chopped
3 cloves garlic, crushed
1 bay leaf
1 teaspoon basil
1 teaspoon oregano
Celery, chopped
Potatoes, cubed
Carrot sticks
2 cans corn, drained
Apples or parsnips, chopped
     (optional)
1 tablespoon cornstarch
     (optional)

Step One: Buy yourself a big hunk of beef. I prefer a boneless cross-rib roast. These are circular in shape, usually tied up with string. Something about slowly heating up this object in bondage works for me. If the roast has a little fat on it, don't put it back; take it home. Fat makes meat taste good and keeps it from drying out when roasted. If you care more about your arteries than you do about flavor, skip this entire recipe and have a bagel with some low-fat cream cheese instead.

Take the roast home. Wash it off. Put it in a roasting pan with a lid. Don't bother with a rack unless you have eroticized dishwashing. Salt and pepper it, and add the whole bottle of cheap red wine, preferably Gallo Hearty Burgundy. (If the wine is sour, add one sugar cube to compensate.) Also add the beef broth, chopped-up yellow onion, crushed garlic, bay leaf, basil, oregano, and some chopped celery. When preparing the celery, take the whole bundle apart. Wash and chop the tender inner stalks first, then add the tougher outer stems if necessary. People are always using the crappy part of the celery and leaving the good part to wilt and rot in their vegetable crispers. Get to the good stuff first, I always say.

Let the roast cook at 350 degrees for 2 hours. Get it out and see if it needs more liquid. If so, add some water. Also add cubed potatoes, carrot sticks, and 2 drained cans of corn (plain, not creamed). You can also add pieces of apples or parsnips, if you like. I usually put 1 potato into the pot for every guest I am having to dinner, plus 1. And I calculate about 2 carrots per person.

Let it cook another 45 minutes to an hour, and it should be done. Put the potatoes, carrots, and corn in a bowl, and take out the roast and slice it. The liquid that everything cooked in should be fine to splash on the potatoes just as it is, without being thickened. But if you feel the need for extra carbs, you can dilute a tablespoon of cornstarch with a little hot water and stir that in to make proper gravy. You'll need to put your roasting pan on a stove burner and heat up the liquid to thicken it. Stir constantly with one of those stupid French whisk things that are so hard to get clean. It won't prevent lumps but you'll know that you tried.

This meal tastes wonderful and impresses dykes who don't know how to cook. The best part of it is that while everything is slowly coming to perfection in your oven, you have a few free hours on hand to do other things with your company. But suggestions about that sort of recreation do not come with this recipe!

Note: If you absolutely must avoid cooking with alcohol, there are lots of ways to make a pot roast taste good. You can put in a splash of vinegar. Cook it with sauerkraut. Put apples in with the onions and garlic, or peaches, to give it a fruity flavor. Dried cherries or cranberries also taste good with beef, I've been told.

Sweet Climax:

Desserts

THERE ARE SOME WHO HAVE THE STRENGTH of will and character to eat their desserts at the end of the meal, after having cleaned their plates and eaten all of their vegetables. I, however, have a sweet tooth, and am happier to begin eating dessert while I've still got room to tuck the stuff away.

So forget a lengthy introduction, and on with the delicious treats (and more seductions than in any other section in the book).

Indulge yourself!

L.S.

Dorothy Allison

Sinful Red Velvet Cake

	One layer	Two layers	Life in excess
Shortening	½ cup	¾ cup	I cup
Sugar	I ½ cups	2 ¼ cups	3 cups
Eggs	2	3	4 small
Plain flour	2 ½ cups	3 ¾ cups	5 cups
Salt	½ teaspoon	¾ teaspoon	I teaspoon
Red food coloring	2 ounces	3 ounces	4 ounces
Cocoa	2 tablespoons	3 tablespoons	4 tablespoons
Buttermilk	I cup	I ½ cups	2 cups
Vanilla	I teaspoon	I ½ teaspoons	2 teaspoons
Baking soda	I ½ teaspoons	2 ¼ teaspoons	3 teaspoons
Vinegar	I tablespoon	I ½ tablespoons	2 tablespoons
Butter flavoring	I teaspoon (optional)		

Do the usual thing to the cake pans with shortening and flour.

In a small bowl, cream the shortening, sugar, and eggs together. In a second large bowl, mix the flour and salt and set aside. In another small bowl, make a paste of the coloring and cocoa. Add buttermilk and vanilla (and butter flavoring if you want) to the cocoa paste. (Call your girl-

103

friend in so she can see how many bowls and pans are sitting around. This way she can later tell everyone how much work you did and give you an instant reputation as a Southern cook of the old style.)

Mix the two wet bowls into the dry bowl very slowly and thoroughly. Do it carefully or you will get red dye all over yourself. Contrary to the usual expectation, red dye stains do not add to your cooking reputation, at least not for the lesbian observer. An exacting talent mixing these ingredients adds instead to your reputation for discretion and attention to detail—highly valuable in some lesbian circles, say Southern California movie and music crowds. Of course, for Northern California lesbian communities, the red dye won't do you any harm at all.

Now comes the most important stage in making this cake. You have one big bowl of gloopy cake mix. The oven is pre-heated. Your pans are greased. To one side, you have your vinegar, to the other your baking soda. Very gradually, you add a little baking soda to your batter, then a little vinegar, then the rest of the baking soda, then the rest of the vinegar. You blend the mixture very briefly and carefully.

Do not overbeat, do not beat hard, just blend. Yes, that's right. This is another of those subtle lesbian tests for sexual aptitude. If you do this right, you will have a pink frothy batter that feels light and cooperative. Do it wrong, and you will have a thick, resistant, gluey mass. Uh huh, there is sexual symbolism in cooking. Absolutely.

Fold the cake mix into the cake pans. Bake in those shallow round pans at 350 degrees for approximately 30 minutes. Be sure and check it with a clean toothpick and if it comes out gloopy, bake some more.

Frost with a plain white icing, so as to make the red stand out even more. Do not add coconut or any tacky decorations. This cake is tacky enough on its own.

If you are feeling particularly evil, use a whipped cream cheese icing (just cream cheese with a couple teaspoons of vanilla whipped to smooth peaks) and serve with strong black coffee.

First Red Velvet Warning: You can never tell how many people are going to want to eat this cake, so my instructions are for a one-, two-, or three-layer cake. The three-layer cake is known as a death-dealer. Women have been known to collapse in sugar shock after eating one too many pieces of a three-layer Red Velvet—so serve it only to people you don't much mind seeing lying gray-faced on a couch.

Second Warning: For best results, you should use red food coloring #2 to make this cake. Red food coloring #2 can still occasionally be found in small ethnic grocery stores. (I recommend Chinatown in either New York City or San Francisco. Haven't tried Chicago's Chinatown. That was the only stop on my first big book tour where no one asked me to cook.) The little bottle you buy in your local A&P or Safeway is not the same. The approved red food coloring has been altered by the FDA to be much less deadly, and equally less effective. For the genuine lurid red dye color, you have to go back to that semi-poisonous old food coloring that only ancient grocery stores or foreign manufacturers will provide. (There is a lesson in this matter for us all. For further information contact your local AIDS organizations that help sick people import low-cost or not-yet-available medications and herbs.)

Third Warning: This is not healthy food. It is never served at the Michigan Women's Music Festival—except for the time I went. This cake is best eaten after strenuous dancing or lovemaking. Never serve after a sultry afternoon meal of pinto beans and greens, or you'll ruin yourself. Never add chocolate chips. Have some respect for tradition.

Final Warning: A woman who would refuse a slice of Red Velvet Cake is not someone with whom you will want to get naked. Too much fastidiousness in food generally reflects a similar problem in bed. Testify.

DOROTHY ALLISON is the author of *Bastard Out of Carolina*, a National Book Award Finalist; *Two or Three Things I Know for Sure*; *Trash*, winner of two Lambda Literary awards; *The Women Who Hate Me*; and *Skin: Talking about Sex, Class, and Literature*, winner of the Lambda Literary Award. She lives in Northern California, with her partner, Alix, and son, Wolf.

Rebecca Brown

*T*he first time I went out with Chris, my partner of four-plus years, I liked her; I mean, I liked her very much.

But I was confused because I wasn't sure if our going out was a "date" or just a couple of neighbors taking in a movie together. We'd played phone tag for a couple weeks, then finally found a time both of us could go to the theater in our neighborhood. So there were a lot of phone messages between the time we'd bumped into each other on the street and the day we were actually going to the show. The more I heard her voice on my phone machine, the more I liked it. So when the day came that we were actually going to get to the show, I suddenly felt weird. I called Helen, my wonderful upstairs neighbor (we lived exactly thirty seconds away from one another but preferred to talk on the phone, which we did almost every day), and I told her I felt weird because I was going to the movies with a woman but I didn't know if it was a date and Helen asked, "Is she cute?" and I said, "She's very cute." Then Helen said, "Are you nervous?" "Well..." I started to say. But Helen heard the pause in my voice. "It's a date," she said.

I knew it was a date when, by the time Chris arrived at my apartment so we could walk down to the theater, I had figured out that I had gotten both the venue and the time of the movie wrong. So instead of a nice walk in the neighborhood, we ended up driving to a theater way across town. Then we had an embarrassing amount of time to kill before the movie. That's when we got in our walk. We walked for an hour and talked about everything. I thought, "This woman is very smart and very cool." I thought, "You can't like anyone so much this quick off the bat..." Then I felt really weird because I was hoping it was a

106

date but I had no idea if it was a date, that is, if she thought it was a date. But I liked her; I mean I liked her very much.

We went to the movie on a Friday. The next day I made my apple pie. It calms me down to bake things, to be in the kitchen and make a big mess and eat good food with friends. When the pie was done I called Helen. I told her I needed to talk with her, and that I'd made a pie, and she came right down. Helen brought some ice cream and we had that on top of our slices of pie. (We each had two slices; it was a good pie.) I told Helen about the amazing Chris but that I still wasn't sure if it had been a date or not, and that, in fact, I actually wasn't sure if Chris was single or interested or—heaven forbid—straight, or just being nice and neighborly. Helen asked me if I had asked Chris any of those pertinent questions. I admitted I hadn't and Helen made this huge Bawk! Bawk! Bawk! Baaaawk! noise like a chicken and told me to get off my butt and call Chris. "Call her right now," Helen said. That sounded a bit rash—terrifying, actually—so I said I'd think about it.

After Helen left, I called another friend, Pat, to get her advice. Pat said to call Chris, but not for a couple of days. Then I called Donna, then Tali, four good chums who have known me for a hundred and fifty years and seen me through a series of affairs too embarrassing to mention. I took my friends' collective advice. I averaged the times they suggested I call Chris and called her at exactly two p.m. on Sunday afternoon. I didn't get her machine; I got her. I bawked out that I'd had a nice time at the movies with her and did she want to see another sometime and—lo and behold—she was on her way out the door to a matinee and asked if I wanted to come along.

I pretended to consider for a second then said, "Sure..." and she came over to pick me up.

The second movie was better than the first.

On the way home to my apartment, I asked if she'd like to come in. "I've got some homemade apple pie," I said as casually as I could.

She pretended to consider for a second, then said, "Sure..." and she came in.

She told me it was the best, the very, very, very best apple pie she ever tasted.

REBECCA BROWN, a former home-care worker, is the author of *The Gifts of the Body*, winner of the Lambda Literary Award, *Annie Oakley's Girl*, *The Terrible Girls*, *The Children's Crusade*, and *The Haunted House*. She lives in Seattle.

The Apple Pie That Seduced My Girlfriend

The Crust

1 ½ cups white flour
1 ½ cups wheat flour
1 cup margarine, room
    temperature
6 tablespoons water

Preheat oven to 425 degrees. In a big bowl, mix white flour with wheat flour (not the real gritty kind, though). Work in margarine. Mush it in with your hands. The best part of cooking is getting all the junk on your hands. Mush it so it's even-ish and sort of sticks together. Mix in, individually, each tablespoon of water so that the dough holds together. Mush it together in one big ball. Then divide the ball in half and roll it out with a floured rolling pin (or a floured bottle). Generously grease a 9-inch pie pan. Put the rolled-out crust in the bottom of the pan. Leave about a half inch of dough hanging over the edge. Leave the other dough in the bowl for now. (This recipe allows for lots of crust so you can bake the extra just to snack on while you're waiting for the pie.)

The Innards

10 or 12 apples, depending on
    size
½ cup sugar
½ cup brown sugar
Powdered cinnamon
A handful of dark raisins
A handful of chopped walnuts
A pinch of ginger
A teensy pinch of pepper
1 or 2 lemons, depending on
    size
1 tablespoon flour or
    cornstarch (optional)
A few pats of butter or
    margarine

Peel and slice the apples. In Seattle, where I live, there's usually loads of windfall apples in the autumn, and I know some good places to glean them. I like gleaned apples because they smell better and taste sharper and are cheaper, but you usually have to buy the apples from a store.

    Put them in a big bowl. Add the sugar, brown sugar, several shakes of powdered cinnamon, dark raisins, chopped walnuts, ginger, and pepper. Squeeze a big or a couple of small lemons into the mixture. Mix it all up. (If you like your pies drippy, this will be fine. If you like them not so drippy you'll want to add a tablespoon of flour or some corn starch to the mixture. I never do though.)

Dump all this into the pie crust. Pat it down smooth so there's a nice round top. Dot the top of the apple mixture with a few pats of butter or margarine. Roll out the other pie dough and place it on top of the pie. Press the edges of the top and bottom pie crust together. Pat the edges of the crust down with a fork and make it cute. Put a few pats of butter or margarine on top of the crust and sprinkle on some sugar and cinnamon. Poke the top with a fork to let out some steam. Be creative. Draw pictures of hearts or write subliminal messages such as I like you. Stick the pie in the oven for 10 minutes. Then reduce the heat to 350 degrees and cook the pie for about an hour, checking on it a few times.

After it's done, take it out of the oven to cool a little. Serve it with ice cream to an old friend or serve it au naturel to a new one.

*Joan Nestle and
Lee Hudson*

The Night the Bowl Sang

Part One: Joan

When Lee first invited me to her Brooklyn apartment for dinner, I knew I would be too nervous to eat. And I was right. I slowly climbed the steps to her door, trying to get myself under control. "Come on in," she called and I stepped into her kitchen, a large open room from whose ceiling hung copper pots and on whose walls dangled intriguing culinary implements—wiry whisks, rubbery spatulas, shiny pastry cones. Now I am femme, but cooking for me was always a matter of stews and soups, chickens and pastas, salads and bread. A wooden spoon was the highest form of cooking utensil in my kitchen. From the public display of her kitchen paraphernalia, I knew I had entered the home of a dedicated cook.

She stood behind her butcher-block island, sleeves rolled up, a white apron folded into a tight band around her waist and hips—"restaurant style" she told me later. All I could think of was a bleached loin cloth. One arm cradled a huge silver mixing bowl, and in her other hand, she wielded a large whisk. Before her stood a good-sized sifter. "Have a seat," she said. "I'm preparing dessert—an angel food cake."

I sat, thinking this is already a cross-cultural culinary experience. I am Jewish, she was raised Catholic. What is an angel food cake? Perhaps something like the sponge cakes we had for the holidays. Then she started whisking the ingredients in the huge bowl. Around and around her arm went, her muscles started to swell, a faint layer of sweat broke out on her forehead. She was explaining to me why she had to beat the egg whites so carefully, but all I was thinking was, please let her save some of that action for me. As the hours went by—or so it felt—I grew to hate those egg whites who were getting so well stirred. I wanted her arm, her hand, even the whisk deep inside of me. How much endurance could she have?

Later in the evening, I learned I had nothing to fear. The cake, so proud on its own special stand, never got eaten, but the whole evening was a work of art.

We have been together for eight years now, and I have eaten many of Lee's angel food cakes. They are light, not too sweet, with a wonderful tang from the orange and lemon topping.

Part Two: Lee

Angel food cakes are healthy, sexy, and devilishly fun to make. Don't be fooled by the name—this is an S/M dessert!

Some say the secret is the air folded in with each brisk whisk stroke, or the timing of the cream of tartar, added during the whipping to stabilize the egg whites as they foam into a creamy pool, or catching that moment when the whites stand in swollen peaks still wet before turning dry, or the gentle-not-too-

forceful folding in of the six-times-sifted flour, or the "extra extra" fine sugar that melts when sprinkled in, or even how slow or hot the heat is when it comes into contact with the batter adding steam to air.

This magical delicate cake rises high between the forceful and the tender: fierce sifting and beating, then gentle folding. Experience helps. As I feel the cake responding with each whisk stroke, slowly swelling with air, I listen to the sound of the whisk snapping and sliding up and down the sides of the large aluminum bowl. Stroke after stroke ringing out. It helps to be ambidextrous so there is no pausing, no chance that the air will escape. It's a wonderful song that thickens as you go.

Just so much good chemistry and music. Like the life I began that night with Joan.

Passionate Angel Cake

1 ½ cups cake flour
¾ cup extra-fine or
    confectioners' sugar
2 ¼ cups egg whites (about a
    dozen eggs)
3 ¼ tablespoons cold water
2 ¼ teaspoons cream of tartar
1 ¼ teaspoons vanilla extract
1 ½ teaspoons almond extract
½ teaspoon salt
1 ½ cups finely granulated or
    sifted sugar

Thoroughly clean and dry a 10-inch tube pan with a removable rim and preheat the oven to 350 degrees. Any grease on the pan will keep the cake from taking hold and climbing up the sides and middle. You will need a funnel or bottom that fits into the top of the pan tube to hold the cake upside down when it comes out of the oven.

First sift, then measure out the cake flour. Add the extra-fine or confectioners' sugar. Sift together 6 times and set it aside.

Next, separate the eggs. In a large whipping bowl, combine the egg whites and cold water. Beat the mixture gently until it is a thickening creamy foam.

Add cream of tartar, vanilla extract, almond extract, and salt.

Continue beating, increasing force and speed while adding finely granulated or sifted sugar until the whites form stiff wet shiny peaks. If you are feeling confident about your performance, it is possible to hold the pan of beaten whites upside down over your head and they won't fall from the bowl. Quickly, firmly but gently, fold in the six-times-sifted flour and other sugar with a rubber spatula.

Pour the batter in the ungreased pan up to a half inch from the top. You may have some left over to put in a small loaf pan to the side. Run the spatula through the batter to break up any air pockets.

Cook about 45 minutes—check after 35 to 40—cake will spring back to the touch, any cracks on top should be dry, and a cake tester (like long toothpick) will come out clean. Let the cake cool for a couple of hours upside down on a funnel or bottle. Take the cake out of the pan with the help of a broad-blade knife gently pulling the cake away from the sides and center of the pan. Turn the cake upside down onto a plate. Angel food cake is traditionally cut with a pronged divider. I'm partial to a semi-sweet chocolate or orange-lemon drip glaze on top.

Orange-Lemon Glaze

1 tablespoon lemon juice
2 tablespoons orange juice
1 teaspoon lemon rind
2 teaspoons orange rind
1 ½ cups of confectioners' sugar

Mix ingredients, and drizzle over the top and down the sides of the cake.

LEE HUDSON left academia, where she'd been a professor of communication arts and American literature, for public service, where she worked for the state in the division of housing and also as a liaison for the gay and lesbian community to the New York mayor's office. With Steve Hogan, she's recently completed a single-volume ready-reference work, *Completely Queer: The Gay and Lesbian Encyclopedia.*

JOAN NESTLE, co-founder of the Lesbian Herstory Archive, is the author of *In a Restricted Country* and editor of *The Persistent Desire: A Butch/Femme Reader, The Penguin Book of International Lesbian Writing,* and the Women on Women series.

Nisa Donnelly

To my mother, food is love and love is healing.

There is no heart so torn, no psyche so shredded that cannot be healed; no micro-organism so evil or strong that it cannot be seduced and conquered. She knows this isn't true, of course, knows the twists and turns and intricacies of life too well; has seen too much mayhem and sadness, illness and death; has shed too many silent tears. But she believes. In magic. In God. In ghosts. In love.

It was inevitable, I suppose, that I, her only child, would come to believe, too. She taught me to see fairies hiding beneath damp leaves in her summer garden. She showed me spirits dancing at dusk, when the sky is streaked purple and gold. We've heard angels singing at dawn, their voices disguised as the cardinal's song, seen the flash of one red, majestic wing against white snow, found an angel's wing-feather caught in a branch like a drop of fresh blood.

I do not speak often of these things. My friends—overeducated, cynical, hard-edged—would not understand. Their world of healing is concentrated on microbes and retroviruses. Miracles come from laboratories. Magic is smoke and mirrors, not angels and ghosts and whisper-spirits. They do not believe in angels. The risk, I suppose, is too great.

"Eat," I tell them, ladling marinara sauce heavily laced with garlic over home-made garlic pasta, "Garlic is good for the immune system." And they laugh. And they eat. And we know the truth and do not speak of it because the truth, like magic, is sometimes too risky to believe. And I have watched the skin pull taut across their fine bones, seen the blue veins show too clearly in their fine, long-fingered hands.

The memory of my grandmother's table and then, later, my mother's at Thanksgiving and Christmas hangs heavily in the air. I no longer wait for official holidays; my friends and I make holidays when we can. Waiting is a risk I am no longer willing to take. "Eat," I tell them, cutting the pie, still warm. The nuts roasted and crunchy. The filling thick and rich, but not too sweet and never runny. It is too fattening, I know that. Overburdened with calories. It cannot replace T-cells or cure lesions or rebuild immune systems, I know that, too. It is only pie, after all, not magic. Except for that moment, that first long glorious moment, when it tastes a great deal like love.

Pecan Pie

½ cup chopped pecans or
   filberts
Southern Comfort or brandy
   (optional)
3 eggs
⅓ cup white sugar
⅓ cup brown sugar
½ teaspoon salt
⅓ cup melted butter
⅓ cup dark corn syrup
⅓ cup light corn syrup
⅓ cup maple syrup
1 cup pecan halves (for top of
   pie)

Chop nuts. If you wish, add enough Southern Comfort or brandy to cover the chopped nuts, and set aside.

Beat together the eggs, sugar, salt, melted butter, and syrups. Mix in the chopped nuts. Pour the mixture into an unbaked pie crust (see below). Arrange pecan halves on top.

Bake in a 375-degree oven for 40 to 50 minutes, or until a knife comes out clean. Let the pie stand before cutting.

Crust

1 ½ cups flour, sifted
¼ cup very finely ground
   pecans
A pinch of salt
½ cup vegetable oil (not corn
   oil)
3 tablespoons ice water

Combine the flour, ground nuts, salt, and vegetable oil; stir with a fork until the mixture forms a ball.

Add ice water and stir with a fork until the bowl comes clean.

Roll the dough out between sheets of wax paper.

NISA DONNELLY is the author of *The Bar Stories: A Novel after All*, winner of the Lambda Literary Award, and *The Love Songs of Phoenix Bay*. She lives in San Francisco.

Barbara Wilson

Ode to Flan

It's custard really, nursery food, and none of its three main ingredients are very good for you: sugar, whole milk, lots of eggs. Yet flan is one of the great desserts of the universe, rich and simple, and very easy to prepare. It is comfort food at its best: milky, soft, and cool; at the same time, it has about it the hint of foreign decadence, the dark complex taste of slightly burnt sugar, innocence debauched. Its place in the dictionary, near flannel *and* flaneur, *suits it perfectly. Of course, it has been around in cookbooks for years as "caramel custard," but that's not the same. True flan is Spanish, or Cuban or Mexican.*

I first tasted flan hitchhiking through Spain many years ago with my friend Wendy. In fact I tasted it every night for about four weeks, the time it took us to travel from Barcelona to Valencia to Alicante, and then inland to Granada and Sevilla, up to Toledo and Madrid, and back to Barcelona. We had a chance to compare creamy flans and silk flans and milky, melting flans, along with tough flans and sticky-sweet flans. Sometimes we had two helpings. Especially in Barcelona, where they called it, nationalistically, crèma catalana. *We needed to be sure it was really the same thing.*

When I came to Granada a year later to study at the university, I found a small flat on a hill with a teeny kitchenette. The stove was powered by a butane canister, and the water came on only twice a day, early in the morning and late at night. Through the window came the smell of garlic frying in olive oil. I ate out mostly, but occasionally cooked up something. One day I had some new friends, English people, coming over to dine, and I thought I would try to make some flan. How hard could it be?

I bought milk and eggs and sugar from the tiny shop on the corner, along with rice and chicken and vegetables from the larger supermarket. I started late and the chicken got a little burnt and the rice cooked too quickly and was watery, so I was harried by the time I turned to my cookbook and opened it up to the flan recipe. Everything was in grams and liters—oh no! Still I managed to throw it together in a bowl. I even cooked up some sugar in a pot, though it was more black than amber. I poured the syrup and then the custard mix into a few custard cups, and then read an instruction that completely threw me: "Place the cups in a baño de Maria.*"*

Maria's bathroom? Maria's bathtub? The custard had to take a shower first? There was no picture in the cookbook, no clue as to what this thing was. Spanish Revereware possibly? But just then the doorbell rang. I hurried the custard cups into the oven and ran to get the door.

They were polite, my English friends. No one commented on the rubbery texture of the flan with its dark syrup like motor oil pooled around it on the plate. Of course, they'd had the chicken-and-rice entree to prepare themselves. And anyway, in England, I told myself, all food tastes like this.

It was years later, when my cooking skills were much improved and I often read cookbooks for sheer enjoyment, that I came across a baño de Maria again. It was nothing more than a bainmarie, a French word that had made it into English, meaning "water bath." Food, custard mostly, is baked in a pan of hot water in order to slow down the cooking and keep the custard soft. Interestingly enough, the word originally comes from the Latin balneum Maria, meaning "the bath of Mary," and Mary was supposedly Moses' sister, who wrote a book on alchemy. Since alchemists sought to transform baser materials into gold, it seems appropriate that flan, transmuted from ordinary ingredients into the elixir of life, is cooked in Mary's bathtub.

There are many ways to make flan. Cubans tend to use condensed milk and more eggs, which makes for a richer texture. Mexican recipes often call for heavy cream and egg yolks on top of the eggs. You can also make flan with pumpkin and cinnamon, a dish reminiscent of Thanksgiving pumpkin pie. I have opted for the very slightly less cholesterol-laden Spanish version. The recipe serves twelve, but my lover and a friend of ours had no problem polishing it off in an evening.

BARBARA WILSON is the author of two popular mystery series, featuring sleuths Pam Nielsen and Cassandra Reilly, as well as other novels and collections of stories. Her mystery Gaudí Afternoon is a madcap romp through Barcelona, Spain, where this recipe (for Wilson) originates. She has also translated various novels, working from the Norwegian, and is co-founder of two feminist publishing companies, Seal Press and Women in Translation.

Ode to Flan

1 ½ cups sugar
2 teaspoons vanilla
7 eggs
½ cup cold milk
4 cups hot milk

Preheat the oven to 325 degrees.

Stir and cook 1 cup of the sugar in a heavy-bottomed enamel saucepan over medium heat until it melts and turns a light amber color. Pour the syrup into either a 1 ½-quart casserole dish or glass custard cups, making sure to coat the bottom and sides.

Combine the vanilla and ½ cup of sugar. Add the eggs and beat with a rotary beater. Stir in the cold milk, then add the hot milk and mix well.

Pour the custard into the caramel-coated casserole or cups. Set in a pan of hot water (2 inches should be sufficient). Bake the casserole for about 1 ½ hours, the custard cups for around 45 minutes. The flan is done if an inserted knife comes out clean.

Remove from the oven and cool first, then chill at least 6 hours. The flan may be turned out, just before serving, onto a large plate or plates. Or it may be eaten, among friends, straight from the bowl.

Steven Saylor

This is a very rich dessert, ideal for holiday buffets and hell on diets.

Cranberry Walnut Pie

1 unfilled pie shell
¼ cup butter
1 cup firmly packed brown
   sugar
3 eggs
½ cup light corn syrup
1 to 1 ½ cups broken walnuts
1 to 1 ½ cups fresh
   cranberries
1 teaspoon vanilla
½ teaspoon salt

Preheat the oven to 450 degrees. Bake unfilled pie shell for 5 to 7 minutes. Allow it to cool. Reduce the oven to 375 degrees.

Cream the butter and sugar. Beat in the eggs, one at a time. Stir in the remaining ingredients. Pour the mixture into the shell. Bake until a toothpick inserted into the filling comes out clean. This will take 40 to 50 minutes, maybe longer. It's a good idea to use a pie-crust shield or foil around the edge of the crust so that it doesn't burn.

STEVEN SAYLOR, an historical novelist, is author of the mystery series Roma Sub Rosa featuring Gordius the Finder, which includes *Roman Blood, Arms of Nemesis, Catalina's Riddle, The Venus Throw,* and *A Murder on the Appian Way.* He lives in Berkeley, California.

Matthew Rettenmund

PHOTO: LORI DEVITO

*E*verything tastes better with Bisquick. If they made Bisquick popsicles, I'd probably try them.

This recipe came from my mother, Linda Rettenmund. She mailed it to me along with some others (that I refuse to give out), which she offered me for my first-ever party in 1995. The party was both a dual birthday for myself and my lover, José Velez, and our ten-month anniversary, so it was especially cool of my always cool mom to send her love in the form of an extremely fattening dessert.

As a Cub Scout, I actually used this recipe to win first prize at a Father-Son Bake-Off. Of course, we all know who actually made the winning dessert. It was Mommy. That may seem like cheating, but let me clarify: My mom always taught me that cheating was wrong, except when it came to the Cub Scouts, because they always expected too much of a group of suburban rug-rats. I mean, baking? I think we were offered extra points toward some badge if we actually started the stove using twigs and kindling.

Linda's Amazing Coconut Pie

2 cups milk
½ cup Bisquick
1 ½ teaspoons vanilla
¾ cup sugar
4 eggs
½ cup margarine, melted and
    cooled
1 cup coconut

Combine all ingredients but the coconut in a blender (or mixer). Mix on low for 3 to 5 minutes. Pour the mixture into a greased (or buttered) 9-inch pie pan. Let it stand 5 minutes. Sprinkle on coconut. Bake at 350 degrees for 40 minutes exactly.

Serve warm or refrigerate. Mom's had this recipe for twenty years.

MATTHEW RETTENMUND is the author of *Boy Culture, Encyclopedia Madonnica, Totally Awesome '80s,* and *Queer Baby Names*. He lives in Manhattan, where he works as a magazine editor.

Mabel Maney

The Trouble with Tippy

Children made my father nervous, so after I was born he took a job that kept him on the road three weeks out of every month. Not only was my father a purveyor of fine paper products for fast food restaurants, he also sold whiskey that he bought dirt cheap down South and resold at ten percent under retail, out of the trunk of his Buick. "The trick to good salesmanship is in the details," my father always told me. He offered discreet home delivery, free of charge.

For years my grandmother said that someday my mother would change her mind about my father and move back home, but after my mother's sixth baby, my grandmother stopped offering. Instead we'd stay at her house on weekends in twos and threes, sleeping on disaster cots borrowed from the hospital where my grandmother volunteered as a Gray Lady.

My father always remembered to bring presents whenever he came home. Sometimes they were swizzle sticks and humorous cocktail napkins from bars where he'd stop to catch his breath between sales calls, and once it was a Stuckey's pecan log that made us all sick before supper. The best thing he ever brought us was a little Beagle puppy, which we promptly named Tipsy, our secret nickname for our father.

My mother immediately changed the dog's name to Tippy. The first night Tippy howled for hours, stopping only after we stuffed her with bowls of white bread soaked in milk. The next morning, we let Tippy have some toaster waffles with blueberry syrup. She got the syrup on her chin whiskers and later rubbed it all over my mother's ice blue crepe de chine couch, but by then we were all in love. Tippy, like my father, was a real charmer. And she was so little. But not for long.

We soon realized Tippy would eat anything. The miniature apple pie sandwiched between the Salisbury steak and mashed potatoes in TV dinners, peanut butter and banana sandwiches with relish, bugs from under the porch, and once even a whole frozen ham.

She loved to ride in the car, especially when we were going to the Piggly-Wiggly. "Don't let that dog eat our supper," my mother always yelled whenever we heard Tippy rummaging through the grocery bags in the back of our station wagon. Sometimes she'd actually get something good, but she'd just as happily sit there and lick the condensation on the boxes of frozen pot pies.

Every year we dressed Tippy up and took her trick-or-treating with us. She looked especially nice as Tippy the Wonder Dog, in her little blue satin cape. Each year my grandmother warned us about the crazy people who put shards of razor blades in candy, but the only person we had to fear was Mrs. Thornburg down the block, who gave away the best candy but first made us come inside and watch a filmstrip about Christian missionaries in Africa. Then she'd hand us a candy bar with a religious pamphlet wrapped around it. One year Tippy got overexcited and snatched the Baby Ruth from my hand. She ate it in one gulp— holy card, rubber band, and all.

The year I was ten and Tippy was four, we spent Easter Sunday at my grandmother's. My father was on a sales trip and my mother was resting. During church, we left Tippy in my grandmother's green Falcon in a shady spot in the parking lot. After mass, we were supposed to go to the hospital in our Easter finery, to cheer up less fortunate children, but when we got back to the car we found a very sick Tippy squeezed into the back dash, moaning and panting like never before. We had seen Tippy overeat many times, and some grass from the back yard and a big burp always fixed her right up, but this time Tippy looked like she was about to explode.

Strewn throughout the car were the remains of four foil-lined shoeboxes that had been filled with my grandmother's prize-winning sugar cookies meant for the hospital kids. I guess even Tippy had her limits.

"Tippy looks terrible!" we cried. We piled into the back seat, caring little that the contents of our Easter baskets were spilling helter-skelter all over the car floor. My grandmother, a tiny woman with a quiet nature and a tendency to meander in traffic, jumped in the driver's seat and raced out of the parking lot, narrowly missing Mrs. Thornburg. While she sped down Main Street to the veterinarian hospital, my brother tried in vain to feed Tippy plastic Easter grass, but Tippy just turned her head. She was really sick!

Later, after the doctor had pumped Tippy's stomach, given her a sedative, and put her in a cage for the night, my grandmother took us to the A&W Root Beer Drive-Thru for hot dogs and pop. We had ham and scalloped potatoes waiting for us at her house, but we didn't want to go home just yet. Not without Tippy.

Between sips from frosty mugs, we filled my grandmother in on Tippy's long culinary history. "You are never, ever to feed that dog human food again," my grandmother cautioned us. The vet had noticed Tippy's corpulent figure, and had extracted a promise from my grandmother to immediately put Tippy on a slimming diet of low-cal dog food. We listened solemnly while my grandmother impressed upon us the proper care and feeding of a dog. We didn't want Tippy to die, did we? We all cried a little, promised to take better care of our beloved pet, and then had another hot dog.

Before we went back to my parents, my grandmother gave each of us a dime so we could call her in case of emergency. The next day my brother spent his on Tootsie Rolls, but I still have mine.

MABEL MANEY is the author of a trio of parodies of Nancy Drew books, *The Case of the Not-So-Nice Nurse*, *The Case of the Good-For-Nothing Girlfriend*, and *Nancy Clue and the Hardly Boys in a Ghost in the Closet*. She lives in San Francisco.

Mabel P. Kuhn's
Festive Holiday Sugar Cookies

1 cup butter
1 cup sugar
2 egg yolks
1 tablespoon cream
½ teaspoon vanilla
½ teaspoon salt
1 teaspoon baking powder
1 ½ cups flour

Let the butter sit out until it reaches room temperature. Beat in the sugar, eggs, milk, and vanilla. Add other ingredients. Mix well. Add about ¼ cup more flour to make the dough stiff enough to roll out. Chill for 1 hour.

Roll the dough to ¼ inch on a floured board. Cut with a bunny- or egg-shaped cookie cutter. Bake at 375 degrees for about 8 minutes. Cool on wire racks.

Decorate egg-shaped cookies with green-tinted coconut, then jelly beans. Decorate bunnies with yellow- or pink-tinted coconut with raisins for eyes and fruit peel for whiskers. Store in a tightly covered box with wax paper between the layers. Do not feed to dogs!

Michael Bronski

These poached pears are luxurious and fragrant. They are the perfect dessert for a light meal and should be served with strong mint tea or a mild, slightly potent coffee. The idea for this recipe occurred to me as I was making a raspberry-pecan torte and discovered that the flavors went together so well I had eaten most of my basic ingredients before I had even made my bread crumbs. The sweet-sticky pears are wonderfully offset by the fresh berry and nut flavors, and if you serve them with a chocolate sauce (using semi-sweet morsels with added bitter chocolate to cut the sugary taste) you can hide the "seams" that mark where the pears have been cut.

When I first served these, my guests mistook them for cooked pears in a sauce, and when Christopher J. Hogan—noted porn critic and raconteur—cut into his with a fork exposing the deep-red filling, he exclaimed, "Oh, my god, you've gone insane." Alice B. Toklas's noted that her Hashish Fudge (otherwise known as marijuana brownies) would send you into fits of reveries—"almost anything St. Theresa did, you can do better"—and while these pears will not heighten your consciousness, they will supply you with an ecstasy that even the saints would envy.

MICHAEL BRONSKI, once a professional chef, is a longtime gay activist, journalist, and critic. He is the author of *Culture Clash,* and editor of *Flashpoint* and *Taking Liberties.* He lives in Boston.

Gingered Poached Pears with Pecan and Raspberry Filling

The Pears

4 pears
2 cups water
1 cup sugar
2 ounces finely sliced fresh
    ginger

When selecting the pears, any type will do, but they should be firm and not too ripe. They should also be large enough to have ample flesh after being cored and hollowed out a bit.

Peel the pears carefully so as not to bruise them and making sure that the stems stay intact. With a paring knife, slice off a thin section of each bottom so that the pears can stand upright, and then a half-inch from the flat bottom cut horizontally through each pear so that you are left with a sturdy base and an upper section of pear that sits on the base.

With a peeler or a paring knife, carefully core the upper pear sections, making sure that you don't break through, but creating enough room for the filling.

In a pot large enough to hold all four pears and cover them with a lid, begin to boil the water, sugar, and ginger. When the sugar has dissolved and the ginger begins to smell potent, turn down the heat to a simmer and place the pears (but not their bottoms) upright in the pot. Very slowly poach the pears, basting them frequently. You can cover the pot part of the time to help steam the fruit as well. The sugar-ginger syrup should become sticky and fragrant as it cooks and coats the fruit.

Cook the pears for 45 minutes on low heat. A toothpick judiciously used can ascertain tenderness. The cooking may vary on the bulk and the firmness of the fruit. After half an hour, add the pear bottoms, which, being completely submerged in the syrup, will cook more quickly. Add more water (or sugar) as needed. At the end of the process, you want to have pears that are tender enough to be easily cut by a fork. Remember that, once out of the pot, the fruit will continue to cook for a while, so it is better to remove them before they are completely done.

Carefully remove the pears, and their bottoms, with a runcible spoon and place them on a platter to cool. Cook the sugar-ginger syrup down so that it is thick and sticky and when done turn off the heat and let it cool.

The Filling

¾ cup pecans, roughly crushed
I cup fresh raspberries, crushed

With your fingers and a fork, roughly crush the pecans. Add the fresh raspberries. The mixture will be rough, moist and very red.

When the pears are cool, hold them firmly in one hand and gently fill them with the pecan-raspberry mixture, making sure that the fruit does not split or bruise. After filling each pear, attach the bottom to it with toothpicks and reset it on the platter standing upright. When each pear is done, ladle the cooling sugar-ginger syrup over the fruit to glaze it. The syrup will continue to run off and back onto the platter, so this has to be repeated many times. The ginger slices will have become curled and candied; try to ladle the syrup in such a way that they attach themselves to the pears. This looks great and tastes even better.

Let the pears cool for several hours at room temperature. Continue to reglaze the pears as they cool. As the syrup cools, it will thicken and coat the fruit more evenly. They should look shiny and quite pretty. The pears can be served any time after they arrive at room temperature. Remove each pear from the platter and place on a single plate. Be careful because they can be delicate and slippery to manage. They can be served as they are or with a coating of chocolate sauce or a side of minted whipped cream. This is a rich dessert so you may not want to overdo it.

Queer Nibbly Bits:

Defying Category

SOME RECIPES ARE INHERENTLY "QUEER" and defy categories. Such as Noodle Kugel: a pudding that encourages experimentation, and straddles the ground between entree and dessert. In this section, you'll find finger foods and other culinary outlaws, like the white-trash favorite, Frito pie, and Louise Rafkin's recipe for the queer dog.

The following indescribably different recipes are thoroughly adaptable, whether you want comfort food or a walk on the wild side of culinary life.

L.S.

Robert Glück

PHOTO: CHRIS KOMATER

*M*y mother's old-fashioned Jewish pudding is good for brunch, lunch, on a buffet, as a side dish with chicken or (heaven forfend) pork—that is, with light meats. It always disappears, even though, or because, it's not very fashionable.

Noodle Kugel

1 pound medium egg noodles, cooked and lightly drained
1 cube butter
½ cup sugar
1 cup fresh bread crumbs
1 medium-sized can crushed pineapple with juice
2 teaspoons vanilla
6 eggs
¼ cup brown sugar
½ cup granola

Mix the noodles, butter, sugar, bread crumbs, pineapple, vanilla and eggs. Place the noodle mixture in a shallow pan. Mix the brown sugar and granola, and spread it over the noodles. Bake for 1 hour at 350 degrees. When it's cool, cut into brownie-sized squares. Serve this warm or cold.

You can make an unusually savory pasta by altering the ingredients (but not the proportions). For example, use chicken stock, smoked chicken, and caramelized onions, instead of pineapple and juice, sugar, and topping.

ROBERT GLÜCK'S books include the novels *Margery Kemp* and *Jack the Modernist*, the story collection *Elements of a Coffee Service*, and a number of books of poetry. His work appears in *The Faber Book of Gay Short Fiction*, *Best American Erotica 1995*, and elsewhere. He lives with Chris Komater, "high on a hill" in San Francisco.

Surina Kahn

*F*or some people, comfort food is mashed potatoes. For others it might be macaroni and cheese. For me it's Aloo Ghobi. My mother used to make this dish for
me when I was a kid. It's not considered to be a particularly special dish in
Pakistan, where I was born, but I loved it. Then when I was five, my family emi-
grated to the U.S. and I immediately became wrapped up in American culture.
And Aloo Ghobi just didn't fit into that scenario.

I was on the fast (American) track of grilled cheese sandwiches (with
American cheese, of course), macaroni and cheese (preferably Kraft or Velveeta),
and Spaghetti-O's. I wanted to be as American as the kids I went to school with.
But I was constantly reminded how different I was—my mother wore traditional Pakistani clothing; my skin was darker than most of my friends; and of course
our house smelled funny with all the Pakistani food my mother insisted on cooking for us. I, however, was determined to Americanize myself. I perfected my
American accent in no time and then tried to teach my mother how to speak in
one. (She didn't go for it.) Then I begged her to make us American food like all
the other mothers I knew. She didn't go for that either.

Now I'm thankful that my mother instilled Pakistani culture into our lives. I
find myself trying to make up for all the time I spent as a kid trying to reject my
heritage, and one of the ways I've done it is by learning how to make all the delicious Pakistani food my mother used to cook. And since I learned from her, I'm
pretty damn good at it, or at least so my friends say. But one thing's for certain:
There's just no comparison between mashed potatoes and Aloo Ghobi. And I

take great comfort in that.

Aloo Ghobi

5 tablespoons oil
3 medium onions, chopped
6 garlic cloves, chopped
1 teaspoon chili powder
1 teaspoon cumin powder
1 teaspoon garam masala powder
2 teaspoons coriander powder
2 teaspoons salt
4 to 5 cups water
1 teaspoon fresh ginger, chopped
6 ounces tomato paste
4 medium to large potatoes, cut into 1-inch squares
1 head cauliflower, cut into florets
1 pound bag frozen green peas

Heat the oil in a large pot on medium-high to high heat. Add the chopped onions, stirring regularly until they are browned (approximately 15 minutes). Add the chopped garlic, spices, and ½ cup water stirring regularly. Add another cup or two of water as needed. The mixture should be moist so the spices are boiling. Eventually you will see a separation of oil and water (after approximately 15 to 20 minutes). The mixture should look like a brown sauce (and smell delicious). This is your masala—the foundation to any good Indian/Pakistani cooking.

Add the ginger, tomato paste, and another cup of water, stirring regularly. Bring to a boil (approximately 5 to 10 minutes). Add the potatoes and another cup water, cover, and bring to a boil, stirring occasionally. Turn the heat down to medium and let it cook for about 10 minutes, stirring occasionally. Add the cauliflower and cook for about 45 minutes (or until cauliflower and potatoes are tender) on medium heat, stirring occasionally. Add the peas, stir, and let cook about 5 minutes. Turn down the heat to medium-low and let it sit until ready to serve.

Serve with Basmati rice or hot Nan or pita bread. Serves six to eight.

Note: You can use less or more of the spices, depending on your taste. But keep this basic formula: Use double the coriander in relation to the other spices; so for example, if you use ½ teaspoon cumin, garam masala, and chili powder, then use 1 teaspoon coriander. These spices can be found at any Indian store (if not at your local market).

SURINA KAHN is a journalist and activist, and past publisher of *Metroline*, the queer paper for Connecticut and Western Massachusetts.

Karen X. Tulchinsky

*D*ecember. While others dream of a white Christmas, shop until they drop, and fret over whether or not to visit their families, I go to the store, buy a ten-pound bag of potatoes, a gallon of oil, and a dozen eggs. That part is easy. Next I need matzo meal, which if I lived in a large eastern city, like New York for example, would be simple.

However, I don't. I live in Vancouver, just above Seattle, on the west coast of Canada, a beautiful city, but not especially known for having a large Jewish population. There is only one Jewish deli in Vancouver, one Jewish bookstore (which also doubles as a gift shop), and one Jewish bakery. In the deli, on a good week, you can sometimes find matzo meal, but not always. If I can't find matzo meal, I'll substitute flour. (Although my bubbe, may she rest in peace, might turn over in her grave, but what choice do I have?)

There is no big mystery to potato latkes. Other than, the greasier the better.

It is traditional to eat latkes during Chanukah (in Ashkenazi circles—Sephardic Jews prefer donuts). It is also traditional to drink sweet red Manishevitz kosher wine, which tastes strangely similar to Robitussin cough syrup. I don't recommend Manishevitz with latkes, unless you were raised in an orthodox Jewish family and are feeling nostalgic. A nice dry French or Australian Cabernet Sauvignon might cut the grease a little more effectively.

Speaking of nostalgia, you might find a sudden urge to call your mother or grandmother while making latkes. You may even hear their voices inside your head saying something like, "Mr. Big Shot. Makes his own latkes now. Very nice. But does he ever think to pick up the phone and call his only mother?"

If this happens, resist the temptation to call her. Instead you might try calling a Jewish friend and inviting him over. You can both talk about your mothers and feed your urge for nostalgia, without having to take a little guilt on the side.

Keep a roll of Tums on hand, or a packet of Alka Selzter. In some cases, latkes have been known to cause heartburn.

KAREN X. TULCHINSKY is the author of *In Her Nature*, and co-editor of *Queer View Mirror: Lesbian and Gay Short Short Fiction* and *Tangled Sheets: Stories and Poems of Lesbian Lust*. She is a Jewish dyke writer who lives in Vancouver, Canada.

Potato Latkes

6 medium-sized potatoes
1 onion
3 eggs
¼ cup matzo meal
1 teaspoon baking soda
1 tablespoon oil, plus oil for
  frying
Salt and pepper
Sour cream (optional)
Sugar and cinnamon
  (optional)

Peel the potatoes and toss them into a large bowl filled with cold water (so they should-n't turn brown). When all six are peeled, cut them into quarters, and then grate them. (I used to grate by hand, although for obvious reasons, I don't recommend it.) Now, I borrow a Cuisinart from one of my fag friends, all of whom have one.

Grate the onion and add it to the grated potatoes. Add the eggs and the matzo meal (or flour if you must), baking soda, and, believe it or not, a tablespoon of oil (I told you they have to be greasy to be good). Add a few pinches of salt and pepper and mix it all together thoroughly.

Heat a lot of oil in a frying pan. Take a handful of batter, squeeze out as much water as possible, form it into a pancake, and plop into the hot oil. Use a spatula to flatten it down. Fry until golden brown, then flip it and cook the other side until brown. Keep adding oil to the pan.

Lay the finished latkes out on a paper towel to soak up at least some of the surface grease—you don't want to keel over from a heart attack after your first bite. Serve with a tablespoon of sour cream, topped with a sugar and cinnamon mixture.

Ess gezunterhait, *eat in good health.*

Tanya Huff

Coleslaw for the Queen

I used to cook a lot but that was mostly because I used to be a cook in the Canadian Naval Reserve. When I signed on, in 1976, they'd just opened the trade to women. Up until then, they'd thought we weren't capable of asking for assistance in moving a fifty-gallon kettle of soup. Well, that's what they must've thought, because heavy lifting was the reason they gave for keeping women out of the trade.

One of the perks of being a Navy cook is that they don't stand parade, so while my fellow reservists were standing at attention in the rain, I was dry and warm inside, making coleslaw for the Queen.

Statistically, this probably wasn't the first queen I'd made coleslaw for, but she was the first accompanied by the Secret Service. Or MI-5. Or whoever those guys in dark suits were. Possibly the Blues Brothers. Every cook in the galley that day had a Suit of his own. Mine stood behind me while I grated cabbage. Nice job if you can get it. I have no idea if Her Majesty actually ate any of the coleslaw, but as this happened some years ago, I doubt indigestion can be blamed for the current state of the Royal Family.

What follows is not a coleslaw recipe.

I don't actually cook much anymore, but I do garden. For much of the summer I'm buried under fresh produce, so instead of cooking, I preserve. Think of this as the hundred-and-second thing to do with a cucumber....

TANYA HUFF is the author of numerous fantasy novels, including *Blood Price, Child of the Grove, Sing the Four Quarters, The Fire's Stone,* and *Gate of Darkness, Circle of Light,* among others. She lives in Ontario, Canada.

The World's Easiest Garlic Dills

Ingredients

40 pickling cucumbers (about 4 pounds) — Okay, I live in the country so I grow my own, but it's been my experience that most grocery stores in Greek, Italian, or Portuguese neighborhoods get bushels of pickling cucumbers every July or August. (Extend the season the further south you are.) If you have room to grow your own, I recommend National Pickling and that you keep an eye out for slugs.

Coarse or pickling salt — The sort of salt you find on those great soft pretzels you can buy from street vendors outside the Royal Ontario Museum in Toronto. No iodine.

3 cups white vinegar — Flavored vinegars are not an option. Trust me on this.

12 cloves peeled garlic for spicing, plus 2 more per sealer — I did say in the beginning that these are garlic dills.

2 tablespoons mixed pickling spice

1 head fresh dill per sealer — Okay, I can't buy heads of fresh dill either, but I can get fresh baby dill in the herb section of my local supermarket, and if I can get it out in the middle of nowhere, the odds are good that you can. Just snip 1 or 2 fronds off this.

Equipment

4 or 5 quart sealers — Use either the modern ones with the snap lids or the old ones with the rubber rings, it doesn't matter. I use the old ones because I bought ten boxes of them for four dollars at an auction. Wide mouth sealers, however, are much easier to fill.

A water-bath processor — These are large kettles with a basket that allows you to raise and lower the jars out of the boiling water. I don't know about in the city, but all country hardware stores carry them. (Although, in a pinch, you can use your large spaghetti pot with a rack in the bottom and a pair of tongs. The important thing to remember is that the sealers must be covered with at least an inch of boiling water during processing.)

A J-cloth or piece of muslin — A piece of old, recently washed curtain sheer works, too, but it must be a type of fabric loose enough to allow the liquid to pass through freely but not so loose that the spices spill out.

A large kettle — I use the enamel pot I actually bought for corn on the cob.

Make a brine of 1 cup salt to 8 cups water. For 1 batch of cucumbers, I usually need to make 2 batches of brine: 2 cups salt, 16 cups water.

Wash the cucumbers thoroughly. Remove all of the blossoms. Soak the cucumbers for 24 hours, covered in the brine.

Remove the cucumbers from the brine; drain them and pat dry.

Fill the water-bath processor with water and begin to heat it. By the time you're ready to use it, the water should be boiling.

Mix the vinegar and 5 cups water in the large kettle. (The proportions, 3 cups vinegar to 5 cups water are what's important here. You may have to add more, depending on the size of your cucumbers. If you do, don't worry about it. These pickles are almost impossible to screw up.)

Tie the 12 cloves of garlic and the pickling spice in the cloth. Add it to the mixture in the kettle.

Bring to a boil.

Add the cucumbers and remove them from the heat.

Place 2 cloves of garlic and the dill in each clean, hot jar. Slow rinsing clean jars with boiling water is the easiest way to both heat and sterilize.

Pack the cucumbers in the jars. Note: pack, not cram. This is why you have 4 or 5 jars. (Occasionally when I've let the cukes get too big, I have 6 or 7 jars, and I call them Polish dills—which, if you've got to buy them, are the best kind.) Make sure you leave a $\frac{1}{2}$ inch of head space between the top of the pickles and the top of the jar.

Put the vinegar mixture back on the heat and return it to a boil.

Remove the spice bag.

At about this point, put either the rubber rings or the snap lids into your water bath (the water should be near boiling by now) to soften the seal.

Pour the vinegar over the cucumbers (I use a soup ladle), making sure the cucumbers are covered, but leaving that $\frac{1}{2}$ inch of head space.

Seal immediately. Note that the rubber rings and snap lids can only be used once.

Process the sealers 20 minutes in the boiling water bath, then set them in a dark place to cool, remembering to leave space between the sealers. Once the pickles are cool, test the seal. With snap lids, there'll be a depression in the middle. With the rubber-ring sealers, turn them upside down and leave them for a while. Leaky pickles can be stored in the fridge but must be used immediately.

Store in a cool, dark place. Enjoy.

PHOTO: CRAIG GOODMAN

Kevin Killian

$\mathcal{I}$ used to make this recipe when I was a child. Unhappy and feeling alone, I would retreat to the kitchen and want some comfort food.

Old-Time Favorites

½ cup butter
1 cup sugar
1 egg
1 ⅛ cups flour
½ teaspoon baking soda
½ teaspoon salt
1 teaspoon vanilla
1 six-ounce package chocolate chips

Preheat the oven to 350 degrees. Cream the butter, then add the white sugar and continue creaming. Add the egg; continue beating until fluffy. Now, add flour, baking soda, salt, and vanilla. Mix well until cookie dough is resilient and sticky. Then add chocolate chips.

This is the basic Joy of Cooking/Fannie Farmer recipe. You can also use the recipe Nestlé provides on the chocolate-chip package, except they use Crisco, if I remember right, instead of butter.

Set the dough aside and get out:

1 loaf Wonder bread (I suppose more vigorous breads could be used, but I have never tried this with anything other than Wonder bread.)
Peanut butter
Grape jam

Carefully slice off (and save) all of the crusts on about 10 pieces of bread. The crusts will be used later.

Mash each slice of bread until it is flat like a piece of paper. (You might try a rolling pin, but I used to use a rolled-up magazine—probably *Highlights for Children*.) Then spread half of the slices with peanut butter and grape jam, and cover them with the remaining slices, so you have apparently five sandwiches. Mash down some more. Then, with a penknife, cut each sandwich into quarters.

Take the bowl in which the dough and chips have been waiting. Combine. You can do this in two ways. Either insert the sandwiches into the cookies or vice versa. But I usually do the former, because putting the cookie dough inside sandwiches that are all mashed flat is hard. Spoon cookies onto greased cookie sheets. This produces 20 pretty fat cookies. Now you decorate the cookies with little bit of the leftover bread crusts...looks very pretty.

Bake cookies for 15 to 20 minutes.

What's good about these cookies, which I called "Old-Time Favorites" (even though I had invented it myself), is the combination of several different flavors that many kids like: peanut butter, chocolate, jelly, butter, and vanilla. They are kind of like peanut butter cookies—but with more flavor. It's like having lunch and dessert at the same time. Kids also like biting into food and finding more—and different—food inside. Adults do, too, we just don't want to admit it. These cookies are absolutely delicious.

KEVIN KILLIAN is the author of a novel, *Shy*; a book of memoirs, *Bedrooms Have Windows*; and a collection of stories, *Little Men*; in addition to numerous plays. He lives in San Francisco.

D. Travers Scott

They used to make a bastardized version of this at the local roller rink: hot-dog chili sauce poured over a bag of plain corn chips. Blech. Here's the real deal, one of my favorite cold-night comfort foods.

Fab Frito ReciPie

1 big bag Fritos, the wide, dipping kind — No, I don't know how many ounces! Just buy the biggest bag they got. No, better buy 2 bags. That way there'll be plenty to snack on while you cook.

1 big hunk yellow cheese (a 1- to 2-pound brick so you'll have plenty left for snacks, nachos, apple pie, etc.) — Not American or Velveeta! They melt too runny. Colby Longhorn is best, or Co-Jack if you're feeling artsy. Cheddar is okay but melts a little clumpy for my taste. If you do get cheddar, use mild or medium, no sharp or extra sharp. This isn't a deli plate you're making.

2 medium onions — Here you can get creative! Red onions will add a nice color, but aren't traditional. Vidalia or sweet yellow will make a sweeter variation, or try your regional favorite. Living in the Pacific Northwest, I use fresh Walla Wallas when they're in season.

Lotsa canned chili — Again, I don't know the specific ounces. Usually 2 or 3 of the large cans will do, but buy more. You always need chili! The absolute best canned chili in the world is Wolf Brand. "How long's it been since you had a big, thick, steaming bowl of Wolf Brand Chili? Well, that's too long!" Unfortunately, it's not available everywhere. If you can't find it, use your fave but remember: NO BEANS!! Chili with beans is an insidious thing. I don't know its origins but I wouldn't be surprised if it was some scam fostered by carpetbaggers.

1 can jalapeño bean dip — You need this to eat with the Fritos while you're cooking.

Okay, short shopping list, huh? Prep is simple: thinly slice or shred the cheese. Chop the onions. Open the cans of chili and bags of Fritos.

You have two cooking options. Baking will make a Frito Pie with crunchier chips, tastier browned cheese, but drier overall and a bitch to clean up. If you use a crock pot or microwave, it will be moister and easier to clean, but all the ingredients will be of an indistinguishable, mushy texture. I recommend baking, but do what ya gotta do.

So take your cooking receptacle of choice and layer the ingredients in this order: chips, cheese, onions, chili. The cheese will glue the chip layer together; the chili will help cook the onions and anchor the layer of chips above. Aim for near-complete coverage in your layers, but don't stress over it. This isn't a Seven-Layer Salad in a glass bowl you're making, no one will see. You should be able to make about three layers of each ingredient (more for crock pots). Top it with another sprinkling of cheese.

Bake (or zap) until cheese is melted through and brown on top. I'd guess 350 degrees for $\frac{1}{2}$ hour. Mom always told me to cook everything at 350 degrees for $\frac{1}{2}$ hour, except meats and baked potatoes, which take an hour.

Serve in individual bowls. No garni. No side dish. Recommend soda, iced tea or beer as the beverage—something to cut the salt and grease.

Vegetarian Version: Rather than veg chili with beans, I'd recommend using veg chili sauce (good luck finding it) or make chili from scratch and substitute fried tofu or crumbled Gardenburgers for meat.

Vegan version: You're out of luck, soy cheese won't melt right.

Lite version: Okay, you can scrimp on the chili. Get some low-fat turkey thang, or better yet make your own using buffalo if it's in season. Do not get low-fat cheese! It won't work, the oil is a necessary bonding agent. Similarly, nix on the baked or lite chips. They don't crunch right.

D. TRAVERS SCOTT is a performance artist and writer, whose work has appeared in numerous anthologies and magazines. He lives in Portland, Oregon.

PHOTO: PAUL J. D'ARCY

Tristan Taormino

Here's my vegetarian version of the famous white-trash dish, Frito Pie. It's basically chili served in a bag of Fritos. Remember that you can make your chili as mild or spicy as you want it, and if this Frito thing doesn't turn you on, then I guess you can just make the chili and serve it over rice.

TRISTAN TAORMINO is the editor of *Best Lesbian Erotica, Ritual Sex, Power Tools,* and various other books, as well as the 'zine *Pucker Up.* She lives in Brooklyn, with her dog, Reggie Love.

Vegetarian-Chili Frito Pie

2 tablespoons olive oil
1 large yellow onion, chopped
6 cloves garlic, minced
3 carrots, diced
1 medium bell pepper,
    chopped
2 to 4 teaspoons cumin
2 to 4 teaspoons basil
2 to 4 teaspoons chili powder
2 to 4 teaspoons salt
1 to 3 teaspoons black pepper
1 to 2 teaspoons cayenne
1 fifteen-ounce can dark red
    kidney beans, drained
1 fifteen-ounce can pink
    kidney beans, drained
1 fifteen-ounce can garbanzo
    beans, drained
1 cup tomato juice
1 sixteen-ounce can tomatoes
3 tablespoons tomato paste
    (half a small can)
1 fifteen-ounce can corn,
    drained
¾ package extra firm tofu,
    diced or cubed
4 small bags Fritos
8 ounces grated Monterey Jack
    cheese
8 ounces sour cream

Heat the olive oil in a medium-sized skillet. Add the onion and garlic, and sauté until the onions are clear. Add the carrots and let them soften a little. Add the bell pepper and about half the desired amount of each seasoning. Stir and sauté over medium heat until all the vegetables are tender.

In a large pot, heat the beans, tomato juice, tomatoes, and tomato paste. Add the vegetables and the corn. Now add the remaining amount of seasonings to your individual taste. Simmer covered over lowest possible heat, stirring occasionally, for 20 to 30 minutes or longer. After 10 to 15 minutes, stir in the tofu.

While the chili is cooking, prepare the pie shell. Take each bag of Fritos and cut them lengthwise and widthwise.

Taste the chili to adjust seasonings. When it's ready, peel back the sides of the Frito bags and pour the chili on top of the Fritos. Serve right in the bag, topped with Monterey Jack cheese and sour cream.

Louise Rafkin

with big thanks to Amy Sabrina

"You are you because your little dog knows you."

—Gertrude Stein

"*It's* the dog or me," many of us have been told.

This is a talk to have with your girlfriend: Who gets to sleep in the bed?

Lucy is a cuddle-bug. Spoons right against me, head on the pillow or resting on my shoulder. Warmth in winter, ticks in summer. A long drink of fur.

"Mohair Palace," my girlfriend calls the bed after Lucy has nested.

We are at a dinner party where three dog owners are defending their sleeping proclivities and three girlfriends are whining and complaining, and ultimately, setting ultimatums.

"I won't have it," says one.

"Not allowed in the bedroom itself," says another.

I'm wincing, waiting for a proclamation from my gal.

"It's hard to put my foot down," she says. "Because their devotion to each other is so deep, and that ultimately spills over to me."

I sigh. Lucy sighs. But one of the other no-dogger's has had the last word.

"Devotion with hair on top," she says.

I Love Lucy Dog Biscuits for Your Beloved Pet

4 ½ cups organic whole-
  wheat flour
I cup oats, or sesame seeds,
  parsley flakes and wheat
  germ for another treat
  flavor
½ cup brewer's yeast
I cup non-fat powdered milk
I tablespoon garlic powder
I tablespoon kelp powder
2 eggs
½ to ¾ cup canola or
  sunflower oil
I cup cold water

Mix the dry ingredients together. Add the eggs, oil, and cold water. Knead the dough for I or 2 minutes, then roll it to ½ inch thick. Cut with dog-bone cutters or cat cutters or people cutters or.... Bake at 350 degrees for 30 minutes or till hard. Don't store these in a warm place, and keep them out of the sun.

Variations: Add a spoonful of peanut butter. More garlic. Whatever your pet adores.

LOUISE RAFKIN is the author of *Queer and Pleasant Danger, Dust to Dust,* and *Street Smarts,* and editor of *Different Daughters* and *Different Mothers.*

Deb Price and Joyce Murdoch

Provincetown has always meant a great deal to us: It was the first place we felt free to hold hands walking down the main (Commercial) street. On one of our evening walks, we came upon the Painted Lady, a Victorian-style house/ restaurant right out of San Francisco. We had a wonderful dinner that late-summer night, including a fabulous appetizer featuring red peppers. While the restaurant didn't last long, our desire for the tasty appetizer did. Here's how we've recreated it at home for our favorite guests ever since.

Painted Lady Peppers

2 large red bell peppers (or yellow or orange, not green or purple)
Olive oil
4-ounce chèvre
6 to 8 basil leaves
12 red or yellow cherry tomatoes (or 1 medium tomato)
12-ounce white cooking wine
Coarse black pepper

Preheat the oven to 425 degrees.

Slice each pepper in half, top to bottom. Remove the seeds and core. Wash well. Rub the outside with olive oil. Press 1 ounce of chèvre into each pepper half. Coarsely chop the basil and place it in the hollow on top of the chèvre. Dice the tomatoes and spread them on top of the basil.

Place the peppers in a shallow casserole dish. Pour white cooking wine into the peppers and add the remainder to the casserole dish. Be sure to add enough to cover the bottom about ¼ inch deep. Sprinkle the peppers with coarse black pepper. Bake for 20 minutes, then baste the peppers with wine from the casserole dish (add a bit more wine if necessary). Remove them from the oven when they are tender (about 45 minutes). Serve on small individual plates.

DEB PRICE, the first nationally syndicated gay-issues columnist, and her partner **JOYCE MURDOCH,** are co-authors of *And Say Hi to Joyce.*

Geoff Ryman

Photo
of Geoff Ryman
unavailable
due to
culinary disaster.

Adventures in Innovation; or It's Nouvelle, but Is It Cuisine?

I wish to share with you some of my great culinary disasters. The full recipes are reconstructed, out of memory, and are offered more in a spirit of warning than of recommendation.

It's like this: I was young. Creative. Not for me the confining limits of someone else's recipes with their false accuracy (have you ever actually used only exactly one ounce of butter?). My food was to be an expression of my unique past: spoiled, living with a mother who always did the cooking.

GEOFF RYMAN is the award-winning author of numerous books, including *Was*, *The Child Garden*, and *The Unconquered Country*. He lives in London, England.

149

Garbage Stew

This was my first experience of rash gastronomic innovation. Not for me a boring old Irish stew. No. Fragrance, I thought, something tantalizingly unidentifiable, subtle, fruity. I grated in a bunch of orange peel among the onions.

Texture, I thought. Something that will buck up the usual glossiness of stew gravy with lumpy meat, something half-way between crunch and grit. I toyed with the idea of Irish Orange Stew Crumble, but discarded it when blinding inspiration hit. I remembered my favorite texture.

Coffee grounds. I put in used coffee grounds.

I imagined that after hours of slow cooking, everything would melt down into an unexpected, winsome creation.

I did anchor myself in an existing recipe for Irish Stew. But I misread it. I thought it said, "Cook at gas 1 for an hour."

It came out smelling exactly like kitchen garbage, only the meat was raw.

I large onion
½ pound carrots
4 or 5 stalks celery
I pound prime stewing steak
½ pint stock (or beer)
Flour to thicken
I filterful used coffee grounds
Peel of I orange
Salt and pepper

Fry the onion until soft, along with the carrots and celery. Brown the meat in the vegetable mixture. Add the stock or beer. Thicken with the flour and then add the coffee grounds and orange peel. Cook at gas mark I for an hour, and serve raw.

Bear Melt

I have always felt that it was a pity that my home country of Canada did not have a more distinctive national cuisine. This vague nationalism, combined with fictionalization and a fridge full of leftovers, became the Bear Melt.

The Bear Melt even had a history. I told guests that the Canadian Pacific railway had been built by crews composed mostly of Chinese and Italian immigrants. Bear Melts had been invented to please both simultaneously.

Essentially, the Melt was a lasagna, filled with quick-fry Oriental vegetables, laced with lumps of old cooked steak, sliced and warmed up, topped off with melted cheese. Again, it was the mixture of textures that appealed to me. Plus, I had a fridge full of old vegetables and tired, cooked meat.

People were exceedingly polite.

Green lasagna noodles
1 large onion
½ pound carrots
4 or 5 stalks celery
Bean shoots
½ pound mushrooms
1 tin (already opened) of
    water chestnuts
1 red pepper
Garlic
"Fresh" ginger
Soy sauce, to taste
Tinned tomato paste
Old, cold, cooked steak
Strong cheddar cheese

Inspect the vegetables. Select limp or tired ones. The mushrooms should be on the turn, preferably browning in uneven patches. The steak should be fridge-rigid from at least a day left uncovered in the refrigerator.

Chop all the ingredients and arrange on plates. Preheat the oven to 375 degrees. Boil the water and set the lasagna noodles cooking. Try to ensure that the lasagna does not cook through and that separate sheets have stuck together in clumps.

Stir-fry vegetables starting with the onion, carrots, garlic, and ginger, and working down to the celery and pepper. Add steak chunks to warm, and soy sauce to taste.

Lay out lasagna noodles in layers with stir-fry mixture and a layer of tomato paste between them. End up with a final layer of lasagna noodle. Top with grated cheddar cheese, and brown in the oven until the lasagna is hard and curly. Take out of the oven, then lay the table, pour wine, pee, wash hands, and call guests. Serve cold.

Paté De Poisson Aromatisé Des Vieux Parquets

This was a catastrophe that was, actually, delicious. The prime ingredient is an old apartment, rising 90 years of age, and a kitchen floor that has been torn up, thus exposing the original shriveled, dusty timber.

The trick is to dump the fish pie all over the floor and hurriedly scoop it back into the dish before guests notice. You must be willing to pretend that the crust is meant to be mixed in with the rest of the pie.

God only knows why, but the taste of really old dust soaked in timber really added something quite unrepeatable to the culinary effect. It was truly delicious, and everyone wanted to know what the secret ingredient was.

Onions
Mushrooms
Flour
Cheap fish
Milk
Butter
Cheddar cheese
Tomatoes
Capers
Potatoes
Bread crumbs
Parsley

Fry the onions and mushrooms together and sprinkle with some of the flour.

Poach the fish in milk. Use the milk to make a cheese sauce. Melt the butter and add cheese and flour to make a paste before adding milk and boiling to thicken.

Put the fish, vegetable mix, and cheese sauce together with cut raw tomatoes and capers into a dish.

Boil and mash the potatoes. Spread on top of dish, and sprinkle with bread crumbs.

Pour liberally over old floor with linoleum recently removed. Scoop briskly back into serving dish with a rapid movement of the wrist towards oneself and into the bowl. Resprinkle with cut parsley, and serve with a flourish.

Tripe Revenge

This is not an example of gastronomic courage, but of simple, bitter revenge. An old telex operator at work, worn out by punching holes in white ticker tape, finally went potty and had his revenge by informing me, beyond any doubting, that the way to cook tripe—cow's stomach to you—is to put it in an oven bag with onions and cook gently for 90 minutes. The results, he said out of pure maliciousness, are really very good.

First off, tripe looks like a cross between a giant oyster mushroom and a sponge cast in latex. Second, it also tastes like it. After cooking, the onions remain raw in the bag, and the tripe itself simply refuses to allow itself to be chewed. It is the only thing I have put in my mouth that I have been completely unable to swallow. (I'm not bragging at this point.)

Tripe
Onions

Put the tripe in a supposedly fast cooking oven bag. Cook for 90 minutes in medium oven. Cook for another hour. Leave in a further 15 minutes. Toss contents lightly in a trashcan and take guests out to dinner.

About the Editor

Lawrence Schimel is the editor of over a dozen anthologies, including *Switch Hitters: Lesbians Write Gay Male Erotica and Gay Men Write Lesbian Erotica* (with Carol Queen); *Two Hearts Desire: Gay Couples on Their Love* (with Michael Lassell); and *Tarot Fantastic* (with Martin H. Greenberg). His own writings appear in numerous periodicals, including *The Lambda Book Report, Drummer, The Tampa Tribune, The Saturday Evening Post, Physics Today, The Writer,* and *Isaac Asimov's SF Magazine,* and in over ninety anthologies, including *Dark Angels, Queer View Mirror, Nice Jewish Girls, Weird Tales from Shakespeare,* and *The Random House Treasury of Light Verse.* He lives in Manhattan, where he writes and edits full time.

Appendix:

Beneficiary Organizations

City	Agency	Address	Founded	Eligibility	Meals per Day	Meal Type	# of Clients Served per Day	Days of Week Meals Served
Atlanta	Project Open Hand	176 Ottley Drive Atlanta, GA 30324 404.872.6947 404.872.9301 fax	1988	HIV/AIDS	800	1 hot dinner 1 hot lunch	400	Mon - Sat
Baltimore	Moveable Feast	3401 Old York Road Baltimore, MD 21218 410.243.4604 phone and fax	1989	homebound with AIDS	385	1 breakfast 1 cold lunch 1 hot dinner	180	Mon - Fri and weekend
Boston	Community Servings	125 Magazine Street Roxbury, MA 02119 617.445.7777 617.445.2444 fax	1990	homebound with AIDS and dependents	300	1 hot four-course meal	300	Mon - Fri
Chicago	Open Hand Chicago	909 W. Belmont Avenue Suite 100 Chicago, IL 60657 312.665.1000 312.665.0044 fax	1988	T-cell below 200; economic or HIV disability	1500	1 cold lunch 1 hot dinner; home-delivered grocery services 15 meals per week	850	Mon - Fri
DC	Food and Friends	58 L Street, SE Washington, DC 20003 202.488.8278 202.488.0851 fax	1988	homebound with HIV/AIDS and dependents	1400	1 breakfast, lunch and dinner	600	Mon - Sat
Denver	Project Angel Heart	Denver Center for Living 915 E. 9th Avenue Denver, CO 80218 303.830.0202 303.830.1840 fax	1991	HIV and diag-nosis	165	1 hot four-course meal; 1 hot nutri-tional lunch	165	Mon - Sat
Los Angeles	Project Angel Food	7574 Sunset Boulevard Los Angeles, CA 90046 213.845.1800 213.845.1818 fax	1989	HIV disabled	850	1 hot dinner 1 hot lunch	850	Sun - Sat
Miami	Food for Life Network	111 SW Third Street Miami, FL 33130 305.375.0400 305.375.8440 fax	1987	HIV/AIDS low income and homebound with AIDS	860	7 frozen meals, 7 breakfasts per week; 1 hot lunch, 1 hot dinner for homebound	550 meals 250 food-bank groceries	Sun - Sat
Minneapolis	Open Arms of Minnesota	PO Box 14578 Minneapolis, MN 55414 612.331.3640 612.331.3356 fax	1987	homebound with HIV/AIDS	80	1 hot four-course meal; 1 cold lunch	80	Mon - Fri

Nutrition Counseling	% Funding Govt. vs. Private	AIDS Funding Title I / Title II	Number of Volunteers	Paid Staff PT / FT	Other Services	Executive Director	Development Director	Client Services Director	Volunteer Director
Dietician	25% vs. 75%	no / no	1500	20	client referrals, newsletter	Loretta Redd	Steve Woods	Linn Maxson	vacant
yes	50% vs. 50%	yes / yes	195	3 / 8	client referrals	vacant	vacant	vacant	Tom Patrick
yes	60% vs. 40%	yes / no	600	13	client referrals	Dede Ketover	David Waters	Gail Hunt	Joseph Cote
yes	35% vs. 65%	yes / yes	650	1 / 5	client referrals, newsletter, nutritional groceries	Sam Clark	Debra Hinde	Ora Thomas	Modesto Valle
yes	15% vs. 85%	yes / no	700	7 / 24	client referrals, newsletter, nutrition counseling	Craig M. Stine	Micki Ballotta	Fay Scattery	Fay Scattery
yes	11% vs. 89%	yes / yes	300	1 / 5	none	Geary Heeley	vacant	Shelley Cohen	Karin Paterson
yes	15% vs. 85%	yes / no	100 per day	10 / 32	nutritional liquid supplements	John Gile	Christopher Hartley	Jenny Ebel	Mark Hartman
yes	100% vs. 0%	yes / no	150	17	client referrals	Peter Ramos	vacant	Christine Stroy-Martin	Gretchen Grey
no	0% vs. 100%	no / no	100	0	client referrals	Bill Rowe	Bill Rowe	Sister Betty Kenny	vacant

City	Agency	Address	Founded	Eligibility	Meals per Day	Meal Type	# of Clients Served per Day	Days of Week Meals Served
New Haven	Caring Cuisine AIDS Project New Haven	850 Grand Avenue Suite 206 New Haven, CT 06511 203.624.0947 203.401.4457	1987	homebound with AIDS and dependents; expanding	45	1 breakfast, lunch and dinner; Full nutrition snacks	45	Sun - Sat
New Orleans	Food for Friends	2533 Columbus Street New Orleans, LA 70119 504.944.6028 504.944.4441 fax	1992	HIV + symptomatic and dependents	450	1 cold lunch 1 hot dinner	225	Mon - Fri
New York City	God's Love We Deliver	166 Avenue of the Americas New York, NY 10013 212.294.8100 212.294.8101 fax	1985	homebound with AIDS and dependents	1800	1 hot lunch 1 hot dinner	900	Mon - Fri
Philadelphia	Metropolitan AIDS Neighborhood Nutrition Alliance	PO Box 30181 Philadelphia, PA 19103 215.496.2662 215.496.1349 fax	1990	homebound with AIDS and dependents	650	1 hot four-course meal	383	Mon - Sat
St. Louis	Food Outreach, Inc.	4579 Laclede Avenue Suite 309 St. Louis, MO 63108 314.367.4461 314.367.8739 fax	1988	HIV/AIDS referred, diagnosed	350	28 frozen meals every 2 weeks; 1 lunch and dinner; nutritional supplements	200	Sun - Sat 2 weeks per time
San Diego	Mama's Kitchen	1875 Second Avenue San Diego, CA 92101 619.233.6262 619.233.6283 fax	1990	homebound with AIDS; HIV symptomatic	338	1 hot dinner 1 cold lunch and snacks	338	Mon - Fri
Santa Fe	Kitchen Angels	500 North Guadalupe Suite G-505 Santa Fe, NM 87501 505.471.7780 505.471.9362 fax	1992	homebound with progressive chronic disease and dependents under 10	60	1 hot four-course meal	60	Mon - Fri
San Francisco	Project Open Hand	2720 17th Street San Francisco, CA 94110 415.558.0600 415.621.0755 fax	1985	HIV + symptomatic	1800	1 hot dinner	over 2000	Sun - Sat
Seattle	Chicken Soup Brigade	1002 East Seneca Seattle, WA 98122 206.328.8979 206.328.0171 fax	1982	AIDS diagnosis symptomatic	500	6 fresh meals delivered once a week	870	Wed and Fri

Nutrition Counseling	% Funding Govt. vs. Private	AIDS Funding Title I / Title II	Number of Volunteers	Paid Staff PT / FT	Other Services	Executive Director	Development Director	Client Services Director	Volunteer Director
yes	30% vs. 70%	yes / no	35	1 / 3	case management, buddy program, support groups, massage, newsletter, psychotherapy	Susan Chudwich	Thayer Quoos	Thayer Quoos	Lynn Torgerson
no	75% vs. 25%	yes / yes	300	3 / 5	client referral	Dr. Michael Kaiser	Jan Berry	Susan Falcon	Noël Twilbeck
yes	32% vs. 68%	yes / yes	2000	21 / 57	client referral, newsletter	Kathy Spahn	Kay Mitchell	Ramon Maldona	Lisa Earlson
yes	26% vs. 74%	no / yes	525	6 / 10	client referrals, nutrition guide	John Barnes	vacant	Danny Smartt	John Green
yes	35% vs. 65%	yes / yes	450	1 / 3	client referrals, newsletter, nutrition center	Mark Utterback	Karen Klaus	Marilyn Goldman	Marilyn Goldman
yes	22% vs. 78%	no / yes	500	2 / 7	client referrals, grocery delivery	Carolyn McFarlane	Ted Roberts	Rue Tootle	Jack Richards
no	0% vs. 100%	no / no	225	1 / 1	client referrals	Tony McCarty	Tony McCarty	none	none
yes	22% vs. 78%	yes / yes	2100	48 / 80	food pantry, groceries delivery, newsletter, client referrals	Tom Nolan	Diana Coleman	Hilda Mercedes	Hilda Mercedes
yes	12% vs. 87%	yes / no	1500	10 / 30	groceries delivery, transportation, housework	Chuck Kuehn	Judy Werle	Jones Linda Pippin	Jones Stebbo Hill

Index

A

acorn squash, 79
    in Swami Shankara's Squash and
        Cumin Soup, Hot or Cold, 23
All-Around Queer Quiche, 88
American Medical Association (AMA),
    22
apples:
    in Apple Pie That Seduced My
        Girlfriend, The, 108
    in stuffing, 84
arroz caldo, 20
arroz con pollo, 21
arugula, 77
asparagus, steamed, 76

B

bacon fat, 29
balsamic vinegar:
    in Fail-Safe Salad Dressing, 43
    in Garlic Mud for Self-Lovers, 40
    in raspberry-jam dressing, 36
baño de Maria, 117 - 118
Barb & Win's Sweet Potato Casserole,
    84
basil, fresh:
    in Anti-Vampire Garlic Pasta with
        Fresh Herbs, 56
    in Green Marinade, 69
    in Laura's Never Fail, Amazingly Rich
        & Chunky Tomato Sauce, 54
    in Painted Lady Peppers, 148
    in Pesto, 37
beans:
    green, steamed, 76
    in Vegetarian-Chili Frito Pie, 145
Bear Melt, 151
beef:
    in All-Around Queer Quiche, 88
    cooking without alcohol, 100
    in Dinner Party Meat Loaf, 97
    in Dream Soup, 19
    in Fell's Meat Loaf, 96
    in Laura's Never Fail, Amazingly Rich
        & Chunky Tomato Sauce, 54

    in Loaves-and-Fishes Almost-Any
        Meat (But No Fish) Meal, The, 94
    Politically Incorrect Pot Roast, 99
Bernard Jensen's Broth or Seasoning, 40
Bisquick, 121
blood oranges, 77
Boston lettuce, 77
breads, *see* cornbreads *or* scones
breakfast:
    Breakfast Cush Cush, 27
    Soft Breakfast Tacos, 85
    tortilla español, 72 - 74
    Whatever Tortilla, The, 39
brewer's yeast, 147
Brianna's Homestyle True Blue Cheese
    Dressing, 77
broccoli:
    in Pasta Primavera, 49
    steamed, 76
Brussels sprouts, steamed, 79
butter lettuce, *see* Boston lettuce
buttermilk:
    in Johnny Cake, 29
    in Sinful Red Velvet Cake, 103
    in Tea-Time Scones, 33
butternut squash, 23

C

cakes, *see* desserts
Campbell's tomato soup, 79
candles, 77
capers:
    in Coq Au Kitty Tsui, 76
    in puttanesca-style tomato sauce, 55
Carother's Olive Oil, 40
carrots:
    in Dilled Pea Soup, 29
    in Grandma Ruthie's Chicken Soup
        for Very Special People, 24
    in Pasta Primavera, 49
    in Seduction Salad, 45
    steamed, 79
Catalonian cuisine, 35
cauliflower:
    in Aloo Ghobi, 133
    steamed, 76
celery:
    in Chicken Rice Stew, 21
    in Dilled Pea Soup, 29

in Grandma Ruthie's Chicken Soup
for Very Special People, 24
Celestial Seasonings teas, 44
chao, 21
cheddar cheese:
in All-Around Queer Quiche, 88
in Fab Frito ReciPie, 142
in Soft Breakfast Tacos, 85
cheese, see specific kinds
cherry tomatoes:
in Green Salad with Blue Cheese
Dressing, 77
in Painted Lady Peppers, 148
chèvre cheese, 148
chicken:
chicken-and-rice pilaf, 21
in Chicken Rice Stew, 21
Coq Au Kitty Tsui, 76
in Grandma Ruthie's Chicken Soup
for Very Special People, 24
in Loaves-and-Fishes Almost-Any-
Meat (But No Fish) Meal, The, 94
Mami's Coke Soy Chicken, 81
roasted, 79
rosemary roast chicken, 97
sauces for, 37, 40
Velvet Chicken, 21
chili:
in Fab Frito ReciPie, 142
in Soft Breakfast Tacos, 85
in Vegetarian-Chili Frito Pie, 145
Chinese cuisine, 21
chives, 69
chocolate chips:
in Gingered Poached Pears with
Pecan and Raspberry Filling, 127
in Old-Time Favorites, 140
cigars, 77
cilantro:
in Soft Breakfast Tacos, 85
in Vietnamese rice chowder, 21
in Whatever Tortilla, The, 39
citrus fruit, see specific kinds
clams, 53
Clarke, Cheryl, 30
clementines, 84
Coca-Cola, 81
cocoa, 103
coconut, 121
colby longhorn cheese, 142
comfort foods:
Aloo Ghobi, 133
Breakfast Cush Cush, 27
Dinner Party Meat Loaf, 97

flan, 119
Old-Time Favorites, 140
cookies, see desserts
coriander, 133
corn:
in Cornbread, 31
in Dream Soup, 19
Golden Bantam, 17
in Lobster Salad for Jim Owles, 67
see also Native American cuisine
cornbreads:
Breakfast Cush Cush, 27
Cornbread, 31
Johnny Cake, 29
Coq Au Kitty Tsui, or Broiled Lime
Caper Chicken, 76
crab, 65
cranberries, 120
crayfish, 65
crookneck squash, 23
crust:
quiche, 88
pecan pie, 115
pie, 108
cucumbers, 138
cumin:
in Swami Shankara's Squash and
Cumin Soup, Hot or Cold, 23
in Turkish Red Lentil Soup, 15
currants, 33

D

dashi, 81
desserts:
Apple Pie That Seduced My
Girlfriend, The, 108
Cranberry Walnut Pie, 120
flan, 119
Gingered Poached Pears with Pecan
and Raspberry Filling, 127
Linda's Amazing Coconut Pie, 121
Old-Time Favorites, 140
Mabel P. Kuhn's Festive Holiday
Sugar Cookies, 125
Noodle Kugel, 131
Passionate Angel Cake, 112
Pecan Pie, 115
Sinful Red Velvet Cake, 103
dill:
in Dilled Pea Soup, 29

in Garlic Dills, 138
Dilled Pea Soup, 29
dog biscuits, 147
dog's diet, do's and don'ts, 124 - 125,
    147
*Dr. David Reuben's Quick Weight-Gain
    Program,* 11
dressings:
    Fail-Safe Salad Dressing, 43
    raspberry jam, 36
    Seduction-Salad Dressing, 45
    Whatever-Salad Dressing, The, 39
duck:
    Newmas, 83
    Peking, 20
dulse, 45

E

Eat More, Weigh Less, 58
egg noodles, 131
eggs:
    in All-Around Queer Quiche, 88
    in flan, 119
    in Soft Breakfast Tacos, 85
    in tortilla español, 72 - 74
    in Whatever Tortilla, The, 39
Egyptian lentils, 15
endive, 45
*Everything You Always Wanted to
    Know about Sex but Were Afraid
    to Ask,* 11

F

fennel, 59
fettucine, 70
filberts, 115
Filipino cuisine, 20
fish:
    marinade for, 69
    in Seafood Paella, 65
    Smoked Salmon and Hazelnut
        Fettucine, 70
    sauce for, 40
    see also specific kinds
flan, 119
flounder, 69

flowers, edible, 88
Flowers, Reg, 48
frisée, 45
Fritos, 142, 145
frittatas, *see* eggs
Front Runner, The, 16

G

Gallo Hearty Burgundy, 99
Garbage Stew, 150
garlic:
    in Anti-Vampire Garlic Pasta with
        Fresh Herbs, 56
    in Chicken Rice Stew, 21
    in Fail-Safe Salad Dressing, 43
    in olive oil, 41
    in Garlic Dills, 138
    in Garlic Mud for Self-Lovers, 40
    in Green Marinade, 69
    in Pesto, 37
    in Seduction-Salad Dressing, 45
    in Whatever-Salad Dressing, Soup
        and Tortilla, The, 39
Gay Activists Alliance, 66
Gay and Lesbian Alliance Against
    Defamation, 66
Gay and Lesbian Independent
    Democrats, 66
ginger:
    in Chicken Rice Stew, 21
    in Gingered Poached Pears with
        Pecan and Raspberry Filling, 127
    in Whatever-Salad Dressing, Soup
        and Tortilla, The, 39
glazes, *see* icing
Golden Bantam, 17
Grandma Ruthie's Matzo Balls, 24
grape jam, 140
Grapes, Blood Oranges, and Kiwi Fruit, 77
grapes, white, 77
Green Marinade, 69
Green Salad with Blue Cheese
    Dressing, 77
greens, *see* lettuces
grilling, 69

Hale, Mary, 11
ham, 88
Hashish Fudge, 126
hazelnuts, 70
herbs, *see specific kinds*
Hispanic cuisine, 21
Hogan, Christopher J., 126
hominy, 17
hot peppers:
    in Dream Soup, 19
    in Soft Breakfast Tacos, 85
    see also specific kinds

icing:
    Orange-Lemon Glaze, 113
    whipped cream cheese, 104
Immune Support Cookbook, The, 11
improvisational dishes:
    Adventures in Innovation, 149
    All-Around Queer Quiche, 88
    Dream Soup, 19
    Loaves-and-Fishes Almost-Any-Meat
       (But No Fish) Meal, The, 94
    Seduction-Salad Dressing, 45
    Whatever, 39
Italian cuisine, 50

jalapeños, 19
Japanese cuisine:
    Mami's Coke Soy Chicken, 81
    notes on, 80
Jewish cuisine:
    Grandma Ruthie's Chicken Soup for
       Very Special People, 24
    Grandma Ruthie's Matzo Balls, 24
    Noodle Kugel, 131
    Potato Latkes, 134

kiwi fruit, 77

lamb:
    in Dream Soup, 19
    in The Loaves-and Fishes Almost-
       Any Meat (But No Fish) Meal, 94
lasagna:
    Mary Louisa, 59
    Trés Gay Lasagna, 51
Lawry's Seasoned Salt, 78 - 79
leeks, 23
lettuces:
    preparation and kinds of, 45
    see also specific kinds
lentils, 15
lime juice:
    in Coq Au Kitty Tsui, 76
    in Green Marinade, 69
    in Vietnamese rice chowder, 21
    in Whatever-Salad Dressing and
       Soup, The, 39
linguini, 53
lobster:
    Lobster Salad for Jim Owles, 67
    tails, 65

Mabel P. Kuhn's Festive Holiday Sugar
    Cookies, 125
Manishevitz wine, 24, 135
marinade, 69
masala sauce, 133
masturbation, 41
matzo meal:
    in Grandma Ruthie's Matzo Balls, 24
    in Potato Latkes, 136
meat, *see specific kinds*
mesclun, 145
Miller, Chris, 11
mint, fresh, 69
miso, 39

Monterey Jack:
    in Soft Taco Eggs, 85
    in Vegetarian-Chili Frito Pie, 145
mozzarella:
    in All-Around Queer Quiche, 88
    in Pasta Primavera, 49
    in Trés Gay Lasagna, 51
mushrooms:
    in Laura's Never Fail, Amazingly Rich
        & Chunky Tomato Sauce, 54
    in Mary Louisa, 59
mustard:
    Dijon, 45
    prepared, 43

N

Native American cuisine, 16 - 17
    role of corn in, 16 - 17, 30
non-fat cheeses, 59
Nutritionists In Aids Care (NIAC), 11

O

Ohrenstein, Senator Manfred, 66
olive oil, tips on purchasing, 40
olives, black, 54
One Is the Sun, 17
onions:
    Bermuda, 67
    in Cornbread, 31
    in tortilla español, 72 - 74
oral sex, 41
orange juice:
    in Newmas Duck, 83
    in Orange-Lemon Glaze, 113
oranges, *see* blood oranges
Ornish, Dean, 58
oysters, smoked, 65

P

paella, 65
Pakistani cuisine, 132
Parmesan cheese, 37

parsley:
    in Anti-Vampire Garlic Pasta with
        Fresh Herbs, 56
    in Mock Gourmet Clam Sauce
        Linguini, 53
    in Pesto, 37
pasta dishes:
    Anti-Vampire Garlic Pasta with Fresh
        Herbs, 56
    Mary Louisa, 59
    Mock Gourmet Clam Sauce
        Linguini, 53
    Pasta Primavera, 49
    sauces for, 37, 54
    Smoked Salmon and Hazelnut
        Fettucine, 70
    Trés Gay Lasagna, 51
    Pasta Primavera, 49
Paté De Poisson Aromatisé Des Vieux
    Parquets, 152
peaches, 67
peanut butter, 140
pears:
    Gingered Poached Pears with Pecan
        and Raspberry Filling, 127
    in Lobster Salad for Jim Owles, 67
peas:
    in Aloo Ghobi, 133
    in Pasta Primavera, 49
    in Seafood Paella, 65
    see also split peas
pecans:
    in Barb & Win's Sweet Potato
        Casserole, 84
    in Gingered Poached Pears with
        Pecan and Raspberry Filling, 127
    in Pecan Pie, 115
penne, 149
peppers, *see* hot peppers *or* sweet pep-
    pers
pheasant:
    in Dream Soup, 19
    free-range, 17
pickles, 138
pies, *see* desserts *or* Fritos
pignoli, *see* pine nuts
pineapple, 131
pine nuts:
    in Pesto, 37
    in Seduction Salad, 45
    in stuffing, 84
    toasting, 46
pork:
    in Dinner Party Meat Loaf, 97

in Dream Soup, 19
in Fell's Meat Loaf, 96
in Loaves-and-Fishes Almost-Any
    Meat (But No Fish) Meal, The, 94
sweet Italian sausage, 54
potatoes:
    in Aloo Ghobi, 133
    Boiled New Potatoes, 76
    in Dilled Pea Soup, 29
    in Lobster Salad for Jim Owles, 67
    Potato Latkes, 136
    in tortilla español, 72 - 74
    see also sweet potatoes
poultry:
    in Dream Soup, 19
    Newmas Duck, 83
    see also chicken
posole, 16
pumpkin, 118

Q

quattro formaggio, 88
quiche, 88

R

radicchio:
    in Green Salad with Blue Cheese
        Dressing, 77
    in Seduction Salad, 45
raisins:
    golden, 33
    in Steamed Vegetables, 79
    in stuffing, 84
raspberries, 127
raspberry jam, 36
red cabbage, 45
red food coloring, 103
red-leaf lettuce:
    in Green Salad with Blue Cheese
        Dressing, 77
    in Seduction Salad, 45
red wine:
    in Mary Louisa, 59
    in Laura's Never Fail, Amazingly Rich
        & Chunky Tomato Sauce, 54
Reuben, Dr. David, 11

ricotta cheese, 51
rice:
    as an accompaniment, 23, 76, 133, 145
    in chicken-and-rice pilaf, 21
    in Chicken Rice Stew, 21
    chowder, 21
    in Seafood Paella, 65
    White Rice, 76
Roast Chicken, 79
romaine, 77
Romano cheese, 54

S

salad dressings, *see* dressings
salads:
    Green Salad with Blue Cheese
        Dressing, 77
    Lobster Salad for Jim Owles, 67
    Seduction Salad, 45
    suggestions for, 54
    Whatever Salad, The, 39
salmon:
    in All-Around Queer Quiche, 88
    Smoked Salmon and Hazelnut
        Fettucine, 70
sandwich dressing, 43
sauces:
    chocolate, 126
    clam , 53
    Laura's Never Fail, Amazingly Rich &
        Chunky Tomato Sauce, 54
    meat sauce, 55
    Pesto, 37
    puttanesca-style tomato sauce, 55
    tomato sauce for meat loaf, 97
    tomato-tuna sauce, 55
scallions, 53
scones, 33
seafood:
    in Lobster Salad for Jim Owles, 67
    in Seafood Paella, 65
Seduction Salad, 45
Serrano peppers, 85
sexual aptitude, test for, 104
shallots, 70
shrimp, 65
smoking techniques, 69
sole, 69
soups:
    Chicken Rice Stew, 21

Dilled Pea Soup, 29
Dream Soup, 19
Grandma Ruthie's Chicken Soup for
    Very Special People, 24
Swami Shankara's Squash and
    Cumin Soup, Hot or Cold, 23
Tomato Soup, 79
Turkish Red Lentil Soup, 15
Whatever Soup, The, 39
Spanish cuisine:
    flan, 119
    tortilla español, 72 - 74
spinach:
    in Green Salad with Blue Cheese
        Dressing, 77
    in Mary Louisa, 59
split peas, 29
squash:
    in Pasta Primavera, 49
    in Swami Shankara's Squash and
        Cumin Soup, Hot or Cold, 23
    see also specific kinds
steamed vegetables, 79
Stewart, Martha, 32
stews, see soups
stuffing, 84
sugar cookies, 125
Swanson's chicken broth, 22
sweet breads, 32
sweet peppers:
    in Painted-Lady Peppers, 148
    in Pasta Primavera, 49
    in puttanesca-style tomato sauce, 55
    in Seduction Salad, 45
    in Seafood Paella, 65
sweet potatoes:
    Barb & Win's Sweet Potato
        Casserole, 84
    topping for, 40
Swiss cheese, 88
swordfish, 69

in Laura's Never Fail, Amazingly
    Rich & Chunky Tomato Sauce, 54
in Mary Louisa, 59
in Seduction Salad, 45
in Tomato Bread, 35
see also cherry tomatoes
tomato sauce:
    in Dinner Party Meat Loaf Sauce, 97
    freezing, 55
    Laura's Never Fail, Amazingly Rich &
        Chunky Tomato Sauce, 54
tortillas, see eggs
Tripe Revenge, 153
tuna:
    suggested sauce for, 69
    in Laura's Never Fail, Amazingly
        Rich & Chunky Tomato Sauce, 54
turkey, 88
Turkish cuisine, 15

V

veal, 55
vegetables, steamed, 76, 79
    suggested sauce for, 40
vegetarian dishes:
    All-Around Queer Quiche, 88
    Aloo Ghobi, 133
    Anti-Vampire Garlic Pasta with Fresh
        Herbs, 56
    Mary Louisa, 59
    Pasta Primavera, 49
    Vegetarian-Chili Frito Pie, 145
    see also specific vegetables
Velvet Chicken, 21
venison, 19
Vermont maple syrup, 31
Vietnamese cuisine, 21
vinegar, see balsamic or white

T

tacos, 85
tangerines, 84
tilapia, 69
Toklas, Alice B., 126
Tomato Soup, 79
tomatoes:
    in Dream Soup, 19

W

walnuts:
    in Apple Pie That Seduced My
        Girlfriend, The, 108
    in Cranberry Walnut Pie, 120
water bath, 119, 138
watercress, 45

Whatever-Salad Dressing, The, 39
Whatever Soup, The, 39
Whatever Tortilla, The, 39
White Rice, 76
white-trash cuisine, 144
white vinegar, 138
white wine:
     in Mock Gourmet Clam Sauce
          Linguini, 53
     in Seafood Paella, 65
Wolf brand chili, 142
Wonder bread, 140

y

yellow squash, 59

z

zucchini:
     in Mary Louisa, 59
     in Pasta Primavera, 49

Books from Cleis Press

DEBUT NOVELS

Memory Mambo by Achy Obejas.
ISBN: 1-57344-017-5 $12.95 paper.

*We Came All The Way from Cuba So
You Could Dress Like This?: Stories*
by Achy Obejas.
ISBN: 0-939416-93-X $10.95 paper.

Seeing Dell by Carol Guess
ISBN: 1-57344-023-X $12.95 paper.

WORLD LITERATURE

A Forbidden Passion by Cristina Peri Rossi.
ISBN: 0-939416-68-9 $9.95 paper.

*Half a Revolution: Contemporary Fiction
by Russian Women,*
edited by Masha Gessen.
ISBN 1-57344-006-X $12.95 paper.

*The Little School: Tales of Disappearance
and Survival in Argentina* by Alicia Partnoy.
ISBN: 0-939416-07-7 $9.95 paper.

THRILLERS & DYSTOPIAS

Another Love by Erzsébet Galgóczi.
ISBN: 0-939416-51-4 $8.95 paper.

Dirty Weekend: A Novel of Revenge
by Helen Zahavi.
ISBN: 0-939416-85-9 $10.95 paper.

Only Lawyers Dancing
by Jan McKemmish.
ISBN: 0-939416-69-7 $9.95 paper.

The Wall by Marlen Haushofer.
ISBN: 0-939416-54-9 $9.95 paper.

VAMPIRES & HORROR

Dark Angels: Lesbian Vampire Stories,
edited by Pam Keesey.
ISBN 1-7344-014-0 $10.95 paper.

*Daughters of Darkness: Lesbian Vampire
Stories,* edited by Pam Keesey.
ISBN: 0-939416-78-6 $9.95 paper.

*Women Who Run with the Werewolves:
Tales of Blood, Lust and Metamorphosis,*
edited by Pam Keesey.
ISBN: 1-57344-057-4 $12.95 paper.

*Sons of Darkness: Tales of Men, Blood and
Immortality,* edited by Michael Rowe and
Thomas S. Roche.
ISBN: 1-57344-059-0 $12.95 paper.

LESBIAN AND GAY STUDIES

*The Case of the Good-For-Nothing
Girlfriend* by Mabel Maney.
ISBN: 0-939416-91-3 $10.95 paper.

The Case of the Not-So-Nice Nurse
by Mabel Maney.
ISBN: 0-939416-76-X $9.95 paper.

*Nancy Clue and the Hardly Boys in A
Ghost in the Closet* by Mabel Maney.
ISBN: 1-57344-012-4 $10.95 paper.

*Different Daughters:
A Book by Mothers of Lesbians,* second
edition, edited by Louise Rafkin.
ISBN: 1-57344-050-7 $12.95 paper.

*Different Mothers: Sons & Daughters of
Lesbians Talk about Their Lives,*
edited by Louise Rafkin.
ISBN: 0-939416-41-7 $9.95 paper.

A Lesbian Love Advisor by Celeste West.
ISBN: 0-939416-26-3 $9.95 paper.

GENDER TRANSGRESSION

Body Alchemy: Transsexual Portraits
by Loren Cameron.
ISBN: 1-57344-062-0 $24.95 paper.

Dagger: On Butch Women,
edited by Roxxie, Lily Burana, Linnea Due.
ISBN: 0-939416-82-4 $14.95 paper.

*I Am My Own Woman: The Outlaw Life of
Charlotte von Mahlsdorf,*
translated by Jean Hollander.
ISBN: 1-57344-010-8 $12.95 paper.

SEXUAL POLITICS

Forbidden Passages: Writings Banned in Canada, introductions by Pat Califia and Janine Fuller.
ISBN: 1-57344-019-1 $14.95 paper.

Public Sex: The Culture of Radical Sex by Pat Califia.
ISBN: 0-939416-89-1 $12.95 paper.

Sex Work: Writings by Women in the Sex Industry, edited by Frédérique Delacoste and Priscilla Alexander.
ISBN: 0-939416-11-5 $16.95 paper.

Susie Bright's Sexual Reality: A Virtual Sex World Reader by Susie Bright.
ISBN: 0-939416-59-X $9.95 paper.

Susie Bright's Sexwise by Susie Bright.
ISBN: 1-57344-002-7 $10.95 paper.

Susie Sexpert's Lesbian Sex World by Susie Bright.
ISBN: 0-939416-35-2 $9.95 paper.

EROTIC LITERATURE

Best Gay Erotica 1996, selected by Scott Heim, edited by Michael Ford.
ISBN: 1-57344-052-3 $12.95 paper.

Best Lesbian Erotica 1996, selected by Heather Lewis, edited by Tristan Taormino.
ISBN: 1-57344-054-X $12.95 paper.

Serious Pleasure: Lesbian Erotic Stories and Poetry, edited by the Sheba Collective.
ISBN: 0-939416-45-X $9.95 paper.

Switch Hitters: Lesbians Write Gay Male Erotica and Gay Men Write Lesbian Erotica, edited by Carol Queen and Lawrence Schimel.
ISBN: 1-57344-021-3 $12.95 paper.

POLITICS OF HEALTH

The Absence of the Dead Is Their Way of Appearing by Mary Winfrey Trautmann.
ISBN: 0-939416-04-2 $8.95 paper.

Don't: A Woman's Word by Elly Danica.
ISBN: 0-939416-22-0 $8.95 paper

Voices in the Night: Women Speaking About Incest, edited by Toni A.H. McNaron and Yarrow Morgan.
ISBN: 0-939416-02-6 $9.95 paper.

With the Power of Each Breath: A Disabled Women's Anthology, edited by Susan Browne, Debra Connors and Nanci Stern.
ISBN: 0-939416-06-9 $10.95 paper.

SEX GUIDES

The Good Vibrations Guide to Sex: How to Have Safe, Fun Sex in the '90s by Cathy Winks and Anne Semans.
ISBN: 0-939416-84-0 $16.95 paper.

Good Sex: Real Stories from Real People, second edition, by Julia Hutton.
ISBN: 1-57344-000-0 $14.95 paper.

COMIX

Dyke Strippers: Lesbian Cartoonists A to Z, edited by Roz Warren.
ISBN: 1-57344-008-6 $16.95 paper.

The Night Audrey's Vibrator Spoke: A Stonewall Riots Collection by Andrea Natalie.
ISBN: 0-939416-64-6 $8.95 paper.

Revenge of Hothead Paisan: Homicidal Lesbian Terrorist by Diane DiMassa.
ISBN: 1-57344-016-7 $16.95 paper.

TRAVEL & COOKING

Betty and Pansy's Severe Queer Review of San Francisco by Betty Pearl and Pansy.
ISBN: 1-57344-056-6 $10.95 paper.

Food for Life & Other Dish, edited by Lawrence Schimel.
ISBN: 1-57344-061-2 $14.95 paper.

WRITER'S REFERENCE

Putting Out: The Essential Publishing Resource Guide For Gay and Lesbian Writers, third edition, by Edisol W. Dotson.
ISBN: 0-939416-87-5 $12.95 paper.

Women & Honor: Some Notes on Lying by Adrienne Rich.
ISBN: 0-939416-44-1 $3.95 paper.

Since 1980, Cleis Press publishes provocative books by women (and a few men) in the United States and Canada.

We welcome your order and will ship your books as quickly as possible. Individual orders must be prepaid (U.S. dollars only). Please add 15% shipping. PA residents add 6% sales tax.

MAIL ORDERS:

Cleis Press
PO Box 8933
Pittsburgh PA 15221

MASTERCARD AND VISA ORDERS:

include account number, expiration date, and signature.

FAX YOUR CREDIT CARD ORDER:

(412) 937-1567

OR, PHONE:

Mon-Fri, 9 am-5 pm EST
(412) 937-1555
or (800) 780-2279

ORDER FORM

QTY.	TITLE	PRICE

Subtotal	
Shipping (add 15%)	
PA residents add 6% sales tax	
TOTAL	

PAYMENT:

☐ MasterCard   ☐ Visa   ☐ Check or Money Order

Account No: _____ Expires: _____

Signature: _____

Daytime Telephone: _____

Name: _____

Address: _____

City, State, Zip: _____

FFL